a thousand voices

Also by Jeri Parker

Uneasy Survivors: Five Women Writers

a thousand voices

Jeri Parker

WINTER BEACH PRESS

Brooklyn, New York • Salt Lake City, Utah
2011

This is a Winter Beach Press Book

Published in the United States by Winter Beach Press,
Brooklyn, New York and Salt Lake City, Utah
winterbeachpress.com

Library of Congress Cataloging-in-Publication Data is available.

ISBN 978-0-9836294-0-5

Manufactured in the United States of America

First Edition

Jacket and interior design by Duane Stapp

For MLS
with a full heart

Teach them to yearn for the vast and endless sea.
—Antoine de Saint-Exupéry

PART ONE

HIS NAME WAS CARLOS. Carlos Louis Salazar. And when his mother had troubles, I more or less stole him. Or that's what I always said. He was the son I wanted, and I did get him for a while.

I didn't say goodbye to him, the boy I called Carlos. He'd made a long and dangerous trip to see me, and the next thing I heard, he was in a coma. I was the one who was asked shall we turn off the machines? and I was the one who said yes. There wasn't a moment of hesitation about having Carlos suffer.

"I'll prepare him for you to come in and see him," the nurse had told me. She took my arm. "To have your goodbye." She was gentle; anyone could see how unprepared I was, trembling in the hallway.

I didn't go with her and look at him dead. "Too much life left in the memories," I murmured, although she couldn't understand me, no one could. I wanted nothing to overlay those memories. I had no use for a word like closure. I was keeping as far from closing anything with Carlos as possible. And then was not the time, irregular as that is. It was the time to be overwhelmed, and exhausted—and yes, frightened.

I don't regret my decision. Whatever I did, it kept him as immediate as a piece of music played for all it's worth, Horowitz playing Scarlatti. I can hear it whenever I want to. Sometimes I get little snippets—a note or two. Sometimes it is an unexpected crescendo sweeping away whatever else makes up my days.

a thousand voices

I'm not surprised that what comes back is everything. But having it extend beyond the sum of the parts that carried us from there to here—does anyone count on such a thing? Maybe if I hadn't spoken at his funeral, I wouldn't have gotten started transcribing all his music.

When I walked to the pulpit, I realized that words weren't necessary. We could all have come up and simply stood together before each other—witnesses. That is what we did afterwards. We stood together—Hispanics, whites, Indians, blacks, businessmen and women in suits, teachers, workmen in green pants and t-shirts, a few babies, quite a few hippies—fellow sojourners. An organ began to play "Amazing Grace," and we started to sing. The spontaneity of it broke what was left of my composure. It was true of everyone, and we stood there singing and swiping at tears and remembering Carlos instead of having coffee and cookies.

Charlie, the son Carlos had fathered unexpectedly, kept coming over to me, shuffling, his head down, reaching for my hand. He was the age Carlos had been when he left my house for the larger world. On Charlie's third pass by, he managed a few words. "I didn't know these things about my father," he said. He could have been Carlos at sixteen—the same cap of dark hair, the beautiful features. "You're Jeri Parker. You taught him." When he looked up, I saw something like amazement in his eyes.

I kept track of what came back to me after that, for Charlie as much as anyone. I didn't make any demands on myself—unities, continuity, any of that—why should I? I just let Carlos take me, as he always had.

"Yes."

HE DOMINATED HIS STREET, what was left of it. To watch him there was to know that he was crazy about being Carlos Louis Salazar.

It was 1964 when I first drove west to find him. I entered a part of Ogden I'd never been in, not twenty blocks from my own neighborhood. His little stucco house sat almost under the cement columns holding up the overpass that carved up Patterson Avenue. It was on the corner of the dead end it formed. If you stepped out of your car, you heard traffic whir by above, sounding like so many wings beating the air.

Life went on unimpeded in the stucco house. It was an indescribable color, not quite white, not sand—the color of wear. Before long it would be turquoise, and that fit the activity on the street. There was laughter and commotion. Dark-skinned, dark-eyed children sat in the driveway, in the sandy yard; they stood in groups of two or three along the picket fence, laughing and gesturing. They played jacks on the walkway below the kitchen window, its white curtains fluttering out over them. They looked like they had been composed for a painting, the reds and greens and violets distributed among them—a street scene in rural Spain, poor and wonderful, nothing to do with this town in northern Utah.

And there was Carlos, doing his famous dives in the sunflowers—the scene that I was to see in my mind again and again. He was small, and it suited him—he made use of his size, flitting and frolicking. He taunted his relationship to gravity; he was Peter Pan on a string, whipped skyward. When he catapulted up, he went farther than he should have, and when he made his arc and came down, he dropped like a stone. He was engaged in his endeavors. He could have been flying a jet for how absorbed he was. But there was abandon too—he'd keep that for another eight years.

His head was going to strike that dirt like a watermelon, I was muttering, as he zoomed down through the extravagant leaves of the blazing yellow sunflowers. Then up he sailed again, and he did that perfect jackknife, even touching his toes before he dropped into the hard dirt. I winced.

Someone came to my car window, but I couldn't look away from the sunflowers. I was expecting to be involved in triage. The scene didn't need a setting to heighten its drama, but it had one. The town was spread at the base of the Wasatch Range, part of the Rocky Mountain Province. Its foothills were not five miles away, soft with newly leafed scrub oak. The mountains rose up from them steeply, carved and sculpted, at first pale green, then gray green, then gray, gray blue, white—1,400 feet of stone and earth brushed with snow. Their immediacy was unnerving to anyone not used to them. The view from where I'd parked was not even interrupted by a tall building.

I knew the mountains by heart, and I felt them behind me. But I hadn't taken my eyes off the sunflowers, their faces as wide as a man's handspan. I began to feel certain that Carlos was down there in the dirt with a head injury when he suddenly appeared on the other side of my car.

He pointed at me and grinned, as if to say *I see you.* I imagined his voice, high, one tone. By then a woman had come out onto the porch.

I got out of the car and walked over to her. "You must be Carlos's mother," I said. She was short and round and curious. That she knew she had been a beauty was in her bearing. She had less confidence than Carlos, but the opinions of the world hadn't mattered to her any more than to him, and I wondered how such a thing gets communicated. She had his same mysterious reserve. I liked her at once.

"You look just like him," I told her, and we both laughed at the supremacy I had already granted the boy who darted past us. "Other way around," I added. "He looks ever so much like you." She glanced down and fumbled with the strings of her red-and-white apron. She was diffident as well as proud.

"I'm a friend of Miss Bentley—Marian Bentley," I said.

"His teacher. She calls here." The quickness of her speech was uncanny.

"She is sick today so she sent me to tell you she couldn't come." I hoped I wasn't worrying her. "She was going to take him for a drive up in the canyon. She didn't want him to be disappointed." I hesitated, watching for a response from Lilly. When she didn't say anything, I told her I would take him if he still wanted to go. "Would that be all right with you?" I asked.

"Does he know you?" She clipped out the words.

"Yes—well, just barely. I met him last night at the school benefit."

"Benefit?" It's indescribable how fast she said those three syllables. It's a very funny word said as fast as possible. I smiled. She went on talking, and all I could do was think about how she sounded. I'd never heard anything like her way of talking. Nothing quite describes her speech—not its rising inflection nor its quality of phrasing everything as a question. There was something satisfying in it, something wonderfully easy that made you want to imitate it. I imagined silver scissors cutting up a strand of taffy, the bits dropping mysteriously into words.

"There was a variety show at the Tabernacle last night to raise money for the school." I couldn't wait for her to talk again, but she didn't say anything so I added, "The big white meeting place across from JB's."

"Oh yeah, Carlos went to that?" she said, quick and neat. Carlos had come over to the porch and she turned and made a few gestures to him. I couldn't understand what she was communicating, but it took her almost no motion and no words. With her hands, her expression, and the slight rise and fall of her shoulders, she carried on a conversation with him. He watched her, his eyebrows lifted. When she turned back to me, she said, "It's okay." She said it as fast as she'd said benefit. By then Carlos was scrambling into the back seat of my car. Like the scent of sunflowers, he seemed almost to come in through the window.

I had no notion how to talk to a deaf ten-year-old, and I couldn't urge him into the front seat beside me where it might have been possible.

All I could do was glance at him in the rearview mirror as we climbed into the foothills and made the turn onto Route 39. Then I paid attention to driving. Ogden Canyon is so narrow that the highway and the Weber River run side by side much of the way, crossing once just before the dam. The road is scarcely wider than the original Indian trail, although that trail followed the top of the south wall, not the floor of the canyon. It would be many thousands of years before anyone paved the bottom of it. The Utes who hunted back and forth along that wall might have captured a boy like Carlos, and his mother as well, and traded them to work in the fields and the haciendas in Mexico.

Carlos was plastered against the window of my old yellow Scout, studying the trees and rocky slopes. He was intent and busy in his observations, flipping from one side of the car to the other in order not to miss anything. He was as lively as the small, darting creatures he saw in the forest. I noticed that he was unmindful of me, and I was glad I hadn't subdued him.

We were in evergreens almost as soon as we left the big homes of the east bench. The turn up into the canyon took us away from city things. Houses and schools and 7- Elevens were replaced by pines and firs and a few spruce. Their canopies sheltered fox and coyotes, moose and bear, as well as squirrels and chipmunks. Mule deer darted in and out of the shadows. We'd see their white tails, and then our eyes would sort the rest of them out from the branches they were lost in. I put the window down just enough to let the tangy scent of the trees and the wildflowers come in.

At the crest of the pass, we parked the car and got out. The air was cool and smelled of damp earth and grasses as well as evergreens. Carlos and I made our way along a mountain trail, and I began to learn what language is and what it isn't. Since my business was teaching it, I was riveted. Those hours of that first day with him reconfigured everything I thought I knew. One observation was how much of communication takes place outside words. The merest movement—no more, it seemed to me, than the anticipation of exchange—brought a nod and grin from Carlos. It was one of the most wholehearted gestures left in the West.

Carlos stopped beside a little yellow flower. I lifted its hood with my finger. "This is the first flower in spring," I said. *Spring*, he mouthed but didn't say. "A yellow violet. We call them dogtooths." I put a couple of fingers over a tooth. "Dogtooth," I continued, and I got down on the ground like a dog. I was laughing; I wasn't so abandoned as to not be dealing with an image of myself on all fours in the grass. "Like the tooth of a dog." I hoped I hadn't knocked the ecstasy out of seeing a delicate little flower. Carlos was skipping and my own laugh changed to a broad smile. I could see he was, if not edified, then not confounded. He was a good player.

We walked to the edge of a meadow and stood surveying the scene below us, perfectly named Nordic Valley. From that height, it looked like an intricate quilt, its pastures and fields making a patchwork of amber and apple green and ochre. The last of the lupines and alpine daisies dotted the hillside. We poked among the trees and flowers. Carlos did such a precise imitation of a squirrel that I leaned against the nearest pine, laughing again, and begged him to repeat it. I had liked nothing better as a kid than to mimic anything that amused me—a duck, a lizard, a stuffy teacher. Here was my match. I suddenly felt a great happiness and clarity.

By then Carlos was digging up a half-buried shell, odd and extravagant there under quaking aspens and pines. He brought his shoulders up, questioning what it was doing so far from the sea, and I wondered not about it or ancient Lake Bonneville that had covered all of this, but about him. How connected he was, in or out of his house on that street at the bottom of the winding road and at the end of the town we'd left behind, a house on a street that was economically isolated from everything above it, that was little more than a barrio. I wondered how he had sprung up from his restricted shore. And I remembered that the early explorers of this land were Franciscan padres, Escalante and Dominguez, sent out from Spain's New Mexico, where Carlos's grandmother was born. He had an older claim to what lay before us than I did.

When the wind began to blow, Carlos tucked his head into his body like a turtle. He had his cap off and his hair jumped out. I noticed how slight he was, how defenseless really, as we ran back to the car.

We drove down the mountain pass toward Huntsville, the river still surging to one side of us. When the road leveled out in the valley, we were in fields and farmland, the glittering reservoir below Pineview Dam in sight. New wheat barely five inches tall lay spread like a pale green blanket almost to the water's edge.

I took a little dirt side road that got us fairly close to a secluded beach on the shores of the reservoir. Carlos had the car door open before I had fully stopped, and he was at the water's edge before I could catch up to him. I was hollering cautions, but then my voice fell silent. I realized it was already extinguished for Carlos—he was now unreachable. If he wasn't looking, he had no speech to read or gesture to take in, as well as no sound to warn. I felt again that overwhelming concern for him and how precarious his route through life would be.

By the time I hurried to where he was, Carlos was sitting in the sand, as natural as water itself, watching the waves come in, one upon the other, and dissolve. Delicate as light, his hand recreated the enigmatic motion of the water rolling and then folding into itself. It remains the only adequate explanation I've had of a wave. "Yes," I heard him say in a high, fleeting voice.

So there he was, the pure thing, exulting in the great fact of life. That was what it was to know Carlos Louis Salazar at age ten. The turn of his head, the great, curious look he spent on everything about him, had disarmed me in an afternoon. I had heard him say one word, but he had a thousand voices I was yet to hear.

"Throw me away!"

I WOULD HAVE SAID I didn't have fifteen minutes a week to spend thinking about Carlos, or being with him, but I found the time. It wasn't easy. I had a heavy schedule at Weber High School. I taught English classes, all the French classes, and I was head of the Language Arts Department. It must have been a series of flukes and shortages that landed me in an administrative position. I'd only been out of college a couple of years—barely long enough to find out what I didn't know.

I think my students liked my youth and energy—and the office I'd turned into what could have passed for a travel agency. They sat around after school looking at the posters of French villages, light streaming across red-tiled rooftops and blue shutters. "Have you been there? Were you right there?" they'd ask. "Yes," I'd say. "I'll take you when you learn French." And they'd ask about *The Rime of the Ancient Mariner.* "Do you really like it?" They'd ask about *The Catcher in the Rye* with a great deal more interest.

I couldn't get students out of my office after school. I'd have to say I didn't quite get it. It was all but my first brush with that kind of popularity. What I remembered of my own high school days was that I was out the door the minute the bell rang.

When I could get away from Weber High the minute the bell rang, I headed down Washington Boulevard to Twentieth Street. I didn't want to lose any time because Carlos wouldn't be at the Utah School for the Deaf after four o'clock. It was an easy drive—straight south along tree-lined streets and moderate brick homes that were losing ground to Taco Bells and gas stations, then east to better-preserved houses with lilac bushes and roses and marigolds in the front yard. I was climbing into the foothills by the time I saw the green lawns of the cemetery. Just across the road from it was the campus of the School for the Deaf. The two-story brick residential halls and the newer classroom buildings formed a quad. Behind them the mountains were enormously imposing. They were close enough that it wasn't unusual for deer to wander down onto the campus.

In that drive was the history of a small town moving away from its blue-collar roots. In one direction was the Army Depot, and further south was Hill Air Force Base—the two biggest employers around. If you went west, you'd be a few blocks from fabled Twenty-fifth Street, home to the Union Station Depot with its gabled entrances and decorative tiles, at one time the center of town. Ogden remained the biggest railroad junction in the west for many years after the Union Pacific and Central Pacific lines joined at nearby Promontory Summit. Al Capone remarked in the twenties that Ogden was too rough for him, and Two-Bit Street, as it was called, was the roughest of all. Buttercup had her headquarters down there as well—she'd made the old Porters and Waiters Club famous. When the opera came to town, she took her ladies; their arrival was more anticipated than the rising of the curtain.

You had to go as far east as you could go to be among the sweeping grounds and well-hidden homes of the Eccles banking family and the Browning Arms heirs. The campus of the School for the Deaf was in that direction but not in that neighborhood. It was lively after classes were dismissed. Parents of local students came to pick them up, and the residential students skipped between dorms and classrooms. I'd walk to Marian's room and hang around talking while she did the elaborate ceremony of closing up for the day. I'd watch her organize the crayons in her box of supplies according to value and hue as well as size. Through it all I was keeping an eye out for Carlos. If I did see him, it was usually for just a minute.

I always inquired about him. "Tell me about the journey Carlos made," I'd say to Marian in our afternoon chats. We'd occasionally go to the Bon Marché for a piece of pie after work, and I'd learn more about Carlos Salazar. "He's traversed the maze of silence, hasn't he?" I remember asking.

"Yes, and he's in the process of matching up speech—which is nothing but arbitrary mouth movements—and meaning."

Those movements that shaped the word *Mama* must have been arbitrary to us, too, when we were three months, six months old. We didn't automatically connect the word and the person. "We never think of the process, do we?" I asked Marian.

"That's right," she answered. "We all performed a miracle when we plucked language seemingly out of the air, but we heard the sound that attaches to an object or a concept."

"Yes, that's what astonishes me. And he signs too."

"They're like two languages to him, and in his case, he's got a third, although I don't know how much his mother speaks Spanish in the home and how much of it he picks up."

I asked Marian when she first taught him. "As soon as no one could handle him," she said. "Everyone wanted him until they had him. You pay a high price for his flamboyance." She spoke of Carlos with a mix of affection and reverence, and since he was all I had ever heard her praise, I paid attention.

"He flew around the room like a little martin when he first came to school," she said in one of our early conversations. "No one knew what to do with him, so of course I got him."

"Did you get all the irrepressibles?"

"I did," she said. "And the intractables. He's got some of that too."

"You taught him to talk, didn't you?"

"I did. At the end of his first year, I wondered if he'd learned one thing. He didn't say the words all my other kids had begun to stammer years earlier: ball, mamama, daddy." She voiced the words in the high, flat, exaggerated speech of the deaf child of that time. It was still more than a decade before technology would begin to change the way such a child could be helped to hear and to talk and several decades before that would all be abandoned for a signing-only deaf community.

"Was he a good student? Was he . . . "

"Smart? Very. Good student? He was a good saboteur. That was his calling. He tried everything a different way from the others, including learning to talk. One afternoon he jumped into the tall wastepaper basket every classroom everywhere has." She paused to gauge my attention. "Always in the back of the room," she continued.

"Heavy metal," I said. "What did he do in there? Was he wearing green?"

"He might have been. It was just big enough for him to get into. If he crouched in it a bit, he was barely visible." I pictured him as she talked. He'd wait, I thought. He'd be sure all eyes had sought him out. Marian's voice guided my imaginings. "Then he sprang," she said, "dark hair flying. His eyes were full of pride—something grander than pride. He could have gone on the stage at any time."

She thought for a moment before she continued. "Triumph—that's the right word. He sprang out of there like a jack-in-the-box. But it wasn't what he did—it was what he said. His voice was nothing but a squeak in those days. And to make it . . ." She paused again, searching for the word she wanted. "To make it extraordinary, it was his first full sentence." Satisfaction was all through her own voice as she spoke.

"He said it from the wastepaper basket?" I asked.

"From the metal wastepaper basket," she answered.

"I wonder how far back they go? Metal wastepaper baskets must have come with the classroom."

"Probably 1884, in this case, when the school was founded. I'm sure they came with the package."

"Thirty-six years after the Mormons arrived," I mused.

"Carlos in the wastepaper basket. It's about him. It's not a history lesson."

"I see him," I said, and I pictured him, slightly smaller.

"It was a dandy first sentence. It would have been a dandy for a hearing child." She was looking toward the window of the classroom, and I could hardly hear her. "'Throw me away,'" I thought she said.

"'Throw me away!'" she repeated, still looking off as she remembered. Her voice was high and ephemeral in imitation of him, the "away" trailing out like a kite tail.

I didn't know anything about the deaf, or teaching them, but I knew that Carlos Salazar's "Throw me away!" would have drifted over the heads of his classmates. And I guessed that if he had had the advantage of hearing, his gift for language might have led him to astonish many more than it did.

"That was really the first thing he said?" I asked.

"Not the first thing," she replied with the impatience I had grown fond of. "The first sentence. He made noises, not like the others—not as much as the others. But deaf children begin a sound at a time, a word at a time, like hearing children. Then one day they combine sounds, and then words."

"Acquiring language," I mused. "Even teaching it, I don't know much about it."

"In the case of Carlos, because his language training didn't really begin until he came to school, it was late. Six crucial years late. He didn't have any language at all when he came here."

I remembered when I'd first seen him.

I was already annoyed with the usual awful rendition of "I Got Rhythm" when I'd gone to the benefit with Marian. Then of course came "If You Knew Susie (Like I Know Susie)." I stated that I only had one medley in me. I tried to whisper, but during "New York, New York," Marian didn't bother to lower her voice. "Remember he's just deaf. You think it will be awkward, but it won't. You know not to fawn over him, don't you? If you reach for him, he'll be gone." When I did see him spring up in the row in front of me and turn, I'd had my inclinations.

In the years I knew him, Carlos almost always wore his beauty like a gift to the world, but occasionally—and regularly when adolescence went through him like a fire—he ripped at it with something like disdain.

a thousand voices

I didn't see him furious until a couple more years after I met him. In that time I often wondered what qualities, or blends of them, would win out in him—the already highly developed daring, the touch of vanity, the intelligence, the gentleness, the fury I guessed was below it all?

There were no such ponderings at first, however. Seeing him festooned in youth and beauty, I had no thought of a flaw in the design. In fact I had to remind myself often that those ears tucked delicately among dark curls could not hear and the unforgettable eyes were already straining to see.

"Home. With."

I CAN SMELL THE GRASS Carlos walked on when I get to thinking about him. A scene will come to mind and I remember the sky under which it took place. He made things vivid—made them fresh and so they stayed vivid. I've added bits and pieces as the years have gone by. Maybe the shifting times shed new light on old memories. However it is, he stays inexhaustible.

He was sick so soon, just a handful more of good years, although he seemed out of reach of any decline at ten. From the first I'd feared almost everything for him except death. He was more otherworldly than childlike, and he carried with him the sense, almost the assurance, of indestructibility.

I wasn't so very much older than Carlos. Twenty-four in my case was more girl than woman. I had some of his daring, and from where I am now, I see that I had some of his whimsy. And like him, I wanted everything—wanted the astonishing blues and yellows of life.

I didn't sort out the reasons why I went out of my way to spend time with Carlos—I just did it. But there were reasons. If I was drawn to him by his charms, I was also undoubtedly drawn to him by what my life as a mother might have been. Looking back, I feel mercy for the woman I was, the woman who wanted everything for the child of great ability and little means.

I wonder if there was another factor I've never thought through. Maybe I was still reaching for my brother, who had floated almost out of the range of retrieval before he ever left St. Anthony's Hospital in Pocatello and came home to us. There were theories—an injection that should have been given just before delivery, not twelve hours in advance, an ice bath to lower a high fever, the fever itself that went on for days. He was damaged, but he was delightful to be with, like Carlos. And at risk. Both of them were discovering the world, and as I watched, I found myself making my own new connections as well.

As I got better acquainted with Carlos, I stopped more often at Marian Bentley's classroom at the end of my own teaching day. If he was around, I was absorbed in his stage shows—that's what they were. Carol Burnett could have taken him right up. He would flash in and out of the doorway for fifteen minutes, never failing to add an installment of his running parody of the school secretary. Ruth was her name, and to see Carlos say *Ruth*, his nose wiggled back like a small pig, was hilarity itself. So was the vigorously huffed sound. Add the pert flip of her head, the pouty mouth, the wagging finger—uh, uh, uh—something flirtatious under it all—he had her, body and soul. It didn't matter who he imitated, he could make two moves and you knew who his prey was.

If Carlos didn't materialize, and that is just the word for his arrival, Marian and I would talk about our work—about teaching a foreign language, teaching English, teaching the deaf. We discussed the gifted student and the student with heavy disadvantages. We talked a lot about Carlos. Everything seemed to lead back to him.

One Friday a few weeks after I'd met him, I got to Marian's classroom later than usual. I was hoping to see his newest charade—part of my fascination was that I couldn't top him—but he didn't show up. "Should we go for pie?" Marian asked. "I know 'pie' means 'soup' to you, but I can get that raspberry."

"Not today," I told her.

"Are you watching for Carlos? Will he be a good son for you?" she asked.

"Oh my, do I look like I need more family?" I replied. It was the kind of reactive thing I said in family-oriented Utah. Even in my early years, I could feel behind schedule, and that would make me flippant.

"You say things like that, but you don't feel them. How old would your son have been?"

"Five," I said.

"Carlos looks about six to you, doesn't he?"

"He's small for his age," I said.

I didn't stay long that day, and I drove away from his school wishing I'd seen him. I hadn't gone half a block when a high croak came from somewhere in the back of the car. It scared me. The second sound I recognized. "'*allo BA-by!*" was delivered at top volume—big accent on the first syllable, Broadway style. A pair of arms crept around me from behind, strong and skinny. Carlos bent his head beside mine and murmured, "Home. With."

I laughed. I wondered what to do. I tried to ask if his mother was expecting him to be home right after school, but he couldn't see what I was saying. He scrambled up into the front seat beside me, and I repeated the question. It failed to connect so I continued driving to my place, which was close.

He approached my house as though he were on a great odyssey. He would have been good in this land in any era, and I thought again of the region's history. I pictured him in skin tents with trappers and traders—Peter Skene Ogden and Etienne Provost, to start with. I wanted to tell him about Jedediah Smith and William Sublette moving among the Utes, exploring, naming. He was heir to that and the only name he would have heard was Brigham Young, a newcomer in comparison; anything more he might have heard would very likely have been negative.

His enthusiasm spilled into a torrent of gestures and sounds. "You!" he said, as though I'd personally designed the street, the lawn in front, the pines that flanked the high house, the brick steps, the home itself. I never admired my place so much as the day Carlos Salazar first walked into it.

"Oh sure, that don't matter," his mother Lilly said when I called her. "He can stay with yous. That's good for him." So the day had those two lovely things—seeing him and hearing her.

By then, Carlos was kneeling before the shelves of books in my bedroom. "All?" he asked and I nodded. "I love them, love their words. I also love your words," I said to him. He took that in. Then he put a hand on one of the books. It was my high school album, senior year. He slid into a cross-legged position on the blue-green shag rug. That was the era—shag rugs and bookcases of pine boards laid across bricks and Judy Collins singing "Wild Mountain Thyme" on the stereo—the mild part of the sixties. I sat beside him as he turned to the back of the book in search of my name. He couldn't find it where he expected it, and he gave me a mischievous look, one rascal to another. "Nothing school!" he pronounced, all his sympathies for the dropout bared.

"I have a different name now."

He thought that over. "Nothing baby?" he asked. It was the first assumption I'd seen him make, although I didn't understand him for a minute. That brief gap before knowing what he meant always interested me. The slight delay let me be more deliberate. "I lost my baby," I told him.

"Nothing love now?" he asked, slipping an imaginary ring off.

"I love someone now," I answered.

"Marry?" he asked, reversing the gesture he'd made with the imaginary ring.

"Probably."

"Name is?"

"You're full of questions," I answered.

"Questions?" He gave me a look of real doubt. "A name?"

"His name is Karl. It's the same as yours, but in English." Suddenly he flew up from beside me. In those days, he never moved slowly. He leaped toward the bathroom, fleet, animal-like. On the way he half turned, stopping before my dressing table to do a ruthless imitation of me noticing myself in the mirror when we'd first come into the room. There were a lot of flourishes in this. Then he became the ruffian street urchin.

I was still laughing when he came out of the bathroom, crossed the long bedroom that served also as a study, bent, now a touch of the lost crown about him, and slipped one hand under the yearbook beside me and the other under my arm and steered us toward the bed. I was trying to say let's go to the kitchen table, but he climbed up on the bed, stretched across it on his stomach, signaled for me to do the same, and opened the book.

I sat down beside him. "Where?" he asked. He couldn't make a *wh* sound and the result was a particularly high-pitched "'ere?" But I understood him. I took his hand in my hand as I'd seen Marian do and held his fingers to my lips and made the sound, exaggerating the *wh* so that he could feel that it was breathed, not voiced. Then I held his finger to his own lips. "Where," he said perfectly. A thrill ran through me. His brilliance in imitating served him well in learning.

I showed him where my name appeared in the index, and he began looking up the pages that were noted behind it. "Too many," he said halfway through his investigation. I tousled his hair and went to fix him a snack.

"That's because it was a small school. We all got to do everything."

When he came into the kitchen, he sat down at the table and picked up the pencil that was lying there. That's when he made the mathematical calculation that is still tacked up on my wall, when he subtracted his age from mine, setting down the fact that I was a little more than twice as old as he was. He wrote his numbers on the back of a picture of me he had found in a photograph album. I came over to see what he was doing.

$$\begin{array}{c} 24 \\ 10 \\ \hline 14 \end{array}$$

Leaning over him, I took the pencil and added the minus sign, wondering how he knew my age.

He'd make a devil lyrical. He seemed more imagined than real—Tom Sawyer, Huckleberry Finn. He was a dazzling creation, preternaturally quick and bright, and he had the kind of unusual beauty you can put up with in a young boy because he was all rip and tear—he wasn't hanging out in front of a mirror. He was conquering the frontier once again, dark eyes seeing it under heavy lashes, offering a broad smile with a suggestion of—what? Irony? His hair curled at his neck. Very few people could keep their hands off his hair. Was it knowing that he couldn't hear that made you want to touch him—touch him in the way of admiring a piece of art that might be lost, might be squandered?

He flew up from the table and reached for the old car horn on one of my shelves. It made a series of silver loops before it widened into a flare. He put it to his lips, tightened them, and produced a great fanfare, as though announcing himself to the world.

"I was trouble in school."

WATCHING CARLOS over the next weeks confirmed my notion that for the child in love with childhood, school is the first bridle. However necessary, it reins the unfettered celebration of life. It reined Carlos like it might have some red stallion. I picture a horse that had never known bit or pace or burden seeking shade under a juniper tree, a dark-haired boy bringing water.

I heard from Carlos himself about the unhappy day when his friend Manuel went to one school and he went to a very different one. It took fifteen years to get the story firsthand. By then I'd put together some of it. His schooling hadn't begun with separation from Manuel and the other friends who came to play on the porch of the stucco house. I've seen photos of that moment—the two boys dressed up and carrying lunch boxes to the first day of class, Manuel hovering protectively. Carlos had no thought yet for the years he'll later sum up as "I was trouble in school."

I met Manuel. I saw him with Carlos, saw a bond that would never be broken, observed how they talked through a private system of inquiries and nods done almost entirely with the eyes, and with instinct flying back and forth between them swifter than any words could have.

Carlos's kindergarten teacher wasn't as able to communicate with him. She couldn't understand why he didn't respond to questions, directions. I imagined her frustration, and her fear—this one isn't mentally right. She did what everyone did then; she sent him to be examined by the school doctor.

"That's when they found out he was deaf," his mother told me. It was said in that almost staccato way of hers. "He must of got that way with that high fever he had. He was real quiet after that, just like his brother. Ernie was worse, though. I think he had the earache too. I was heartsick when I took him home that day."

I found the chance to ask her if Carlos had made sounds or talked when he was a baby. By then I was calling her Lilly, which Carlos often called her himself, interchanging it with Mother.

"No, he never did much," she told me. "He was real tiny and quiet all the time." *All the time* was said so fast I thought again of when I'd first heard her say *benefit.* "The nurses used to try to get him to make some sounds, but he didn't do it. One nurse told me she'd like to pinch him so he'd make noises like the other babies. Those nurses were crazy about him. They would hardly let me hold him. They fought over him, you know?" There was something mysterious as well as rapid-fire in her speech, and I had to concentrate to follow her. A smile came, and the *you know* was said like a question. "He was my most beautiful baby."

"It's nerve deafness," Marian insisted to me when she told me about Carlos being sent home from kindergarten. "Both Carlos and Ernie were born deaf. Two in the same family—it's congenital." She was emphatic. I saw in her the longing to have had a chance with him in those first five years when, for deaf children as well as hearing, the foundation for language is laid.

"Could you have a deaf child for five years and not know it?" I asked in wonder.

"None of us knows what Lilly knows," she said.

Whatever the medical reasons, Carlos was sent home for another winter to run the streets, play in the river down in the gully beyond his house, watch the trains come and go. Lilly didn't send him to the Utah School for the Deaf until the following year. He must have hit the staid brick buildings on Twentieth Street like a stallion. Stories about him were passed up and down the halls by veteran teachers with the nod for what had been endured, and by teachers in training with a shiver for how many boys like Carlos might lay ahead.

One story that was endlessly retold was his escapade in the cemetery—series of escapades would be more accurate. The highlights had been conflated into one long saga. It is true that he never got over loving to lead his class to the cemetery, which was practically just over the fence from his school. His colorful troop would fly out of the classroom like so many low-feeding birds, like magpies. He could tempt anyone into disobedience, and do it any number of times. His schoolmates followed him, sweeping down and gathering bouquets of wilting gladiola.

And—this is the curious part—back they would fly to the campus they had left, a major infraction for which they would be punished. And they would calm themselves, straighten skirt and pant, brush back hair, although the blush of mutiny couldn't be wiped away. Then they would part from one another and walk into their teachers' classrooms and ceremoniously present them with the now-ragged as well as drooping gladiola. How could a teacher respond? It happened over and over, and no one ever figured out how to say thanks but no thanks.

"For you! Miss Bentley," Carlos would say, his face awash in love.

He had combined some elements no one could quite come to terms with. And he had picked the funniest possible flower to hold out like an Olympic torch before him and his regiment.

Once in a ball game he began to run beyond the bases and the whole schoolyard fell in behind him, leaving the game for a better one as they tore in a pulsing line through the quiet streets of brick houses and pines and cottonwoods and sycamores until they reached the downtown area. High with rebellion, they broke into groups and piled into stores, gesturing and crying out to one another in the ecstasies of unexpected freedom. Fifty rings were supposed to have vanished from the rotating racks in Woolworth's, and the boys ended up in the women's room at Penney's.

In spite of—or perhaps because of—his dangers, none of the other children could keep away from Carlos. He magnetized with his changeable beauties—first shy until he wouldn't come out of the bushes and then daring until he had the girls in them.

However cavalier he could be, going off to the School for the Deaf wasn't all a lark. Although there were birthday parties and outings in addition to the devilment he raised, many of Carlos's hours were spent adjusting the clumsy earphones that were used in those days in an effort to improve their reception. He secretly turned the volume down so that the uneven sound went away; he was required to keep them on. As an oral student, he was discouraged from using sign language at school. Every means was deployed to lead him to talk. His teachers held to their vision of what a wider world he would live in if he could speak as well as sign.

Nothing taught me what Carlos was up against in learning language the way trying to teach him did, but by the time I attempted it, his school had had four years to subdue him. After my venture, I could only hold my breath and imagine what his undiluted spirit must have been.

I walked into his classroom full of a sense of self that is an embarrassment to me now. I wasn't one of those teachers whom perfectly nice students find themselves trying to throw out the second-story window, and I knew it. I'd been too fussed over to be ready for Carlos and his classmates. Maybe commanding interest is the worst thing that can happen to a teacher.

I was different when I walked out of Carlos's room. My friend Marian had introduced me to his class, and that meant that every child began by sitting in a state of fascination. She was imposing, and she knew just what she was doing. They looked at her, they always looked at her. They turned their heads to each other when she nodded toward one of them or said, "Bobby is going to answer the question," or "What do you think, Carlos?"

I was prepared with something or other, prepared to answer questions about myself, I guess. I hate to think I had the idea that those kids were going to be enthralled by me. I said something I hoped would captivate. It was probably something like *You look so fine* or *I'm so glad to come here.* If I were doing it again, I'd take in a fishing rod and ask, *What can we catch?*

They turned to Marian. Their faces showed confusion, and unease was right behind it. What I saw, finally, was that their discomfort was for me. I was outside, inappropriate, alone. I had a lot of grit—that's all

I had, and I could at least see that much—so I sat up, I paid attention.

It was too late. I had lost them, and my friend let me fumble for a few minutes as the boys and girls began to giggle, I would even have to say to mock. Then she came down, not with a hand, not with a voice—that would have been nothing—but with a will that would have made Creon shrivel. They looked up, they watched her, they battled again with their terrible necessity to learn language.

I limped out of that classroom. Even Carlos had been mocking. It was they who knew something I didn't know. They were learning how to talk to the hearing, and I didn't know how to talk to the deaf. Their superiority was arrogant; it was dismissing. I recognized it. I'd been on what was suddenly their side of it all my life.

After that I began learning about language and what teaches it. Going over and over French and English lessons, I'd figured out that you provide a pattern, but how could that be done for someone who didn't hear it, didn't yet understand it written? Something broke into my world.

"Language is other people's system, isn't it?" I asked Marian, and I saw in my mind Carlos watching, watching, making his deliberate way into the world where speech is connected to meaning.

"Yes," she answered. "It has nothing to do with him, with the life he's lived and the way he's learned to get along. That is particularly true of Carlos because he was talked to in gestures more than in words."

I studied the technicalities of teaching the deaf—not to instruct a classroom full of students, although I did do that eventually. For now I was not that ambitious, or rather, I was only ambitious for Carlos. So I learned about showing someone to read lips, to speechread, as Marian taught me to call it.

"Only forty percent of the sounds in speech are visible," she told me.

"What do you mean, 'visible' sounds? Show me a sound."

I watched her as she said *five*, or rather mouthed it. She asked me what I saw.

"Well, I did see something," I told her. I went on. "I saw the *f*, the mouth open for a vowel, but I couldn't say what vowel, and I saw another *f*. No, it was a *v*."

"Try this," she said and mouthed another word.

"Pa," I said.

"You had a one-in-three shot at it and you made a lucky guess. What is this?" She formed another word. I asked for a clue.

"Give me your answer," she pushed.

I said, "Pa?"

"No," she answered. "You've run out of luck. I said ma. Here's another."

By then I had lost my edge; I didn't guess, I asked. She said, "Ba." I repeated it, saying the three sounds to myself—pa, ma, ba. "They're the same," I exclaimed.

"Yes and no," Marian said. Marian never said just yes. "What's the same?"

I said them over and over. I thought. "They are shaped the same," I ventured.

"Yes. That's the forty percent of speech that is distinguishable on the lips. The rest is overlap."

"Back to paa, maa, baa." I said them like a bleating sheep.

"Try to take it seriously," Marian said.

"Why don't they sound the same?"

"Think about it," Marian said.

I awoke in the middle of the night with the answer and called her. "Air," I said.

"It's 2:00 a.m. That's right. What about the air?" And she hung up.

I was having fun. I could speculate, I could theorize, I could experiment, but for Carlos, the same endeavor was a race to catch up, to gain ground that would enable him not just to survive but to flourish.

I got so I could talk better with him. Almost at once I could say, "At two this afternoon," and tell if he understood and would be waiting for me. He liked me to take his hand as I had seen Marian do and hold it to my mouth so he could feel the release of air in a sound like *where* or *what.* He'd put his fingers to his own mouth to see if he was replicating it. His *where* was high and mysterious, trailing out like so many of his words did. It was enchanting to hear, and I very quickly realized I didn't want him to get so good he sounded like everyone else.

I loaded the teaching of speech with everything I had in order to keep his interest. I held my ears as though another sound like the one I'd just heard would finish me off when his speech was rough. And I'd faint away in bliss when he said something well.

He played with me too. He would purposely let his speech "go to pot," as I taught him to say, for the delight of seeing me angle away from the sounds. And it touched him—it touched him deeper than the game, and I saw that—when he spoke beautifully.

After a few months, I decided there wasn't much to teaching speech. I hadn't really begun to teach speech, let alone language. I'd stayed in the concrete world and dealt mostly with words Carlos already knew. One day I said, "Let's go on a picnic if the weather is nice." I'd said, "Let's go on a picnic" before. And I knew that maybe the only word Carlos was sure of was picnic. But it had gotten us underway, and when we were in the canyon we could talk about hot dogs and potato chips. But this *if*?

"Eef?" Carlos looked up. I stopped. *If?* I wove myself into incomprehensibility. "Maybe the weather will be fine. Maybe it will be sunny." I tried not to use my hands much, but I had a terrible need to show the sun beaming down on us. Marian considered this bringing a crutch onto the scene. I could see that point of view in a way, but I'd asked, "Don't we both deserve a crutch?"

"Don't talk schools of thought yet," she had answered. "Just don't do it. Make yourself find a way."

"Maybe it will rain," I said to Carlos.

"Meybe?"

"Will it rain? Maybe yes, maybe no. Maybe," I replied.

The discussion ended an hour later, my dark-eyed boy disconnected and uninterested in the picnic. I drew two sketches in a flash. In one, we sat in the canyon eating under a bright sun. In the other, we stood at the window of his classroom, looking wistfully out at the rain.

"If it is nice, we will go on a picnic," I said.

"Oh, sunny?" he said.

"*If* it is sunny."

He skipped out, mumbling "Eef."

"Always remember thees."

LITTLE BY LITTLE, Carlos became part of my life. By the time school was out for the summer, he fit as though he'd always been there. It was as natural and effortless as leaves growing on trees. I'd call Lilly and ask if Carlos wanted to go up in the canyon for the afternoon. A couple of times, she called me and said, "That kid wonders what you're doing."

I was in Ogden Canyon nearly every day once I wasn't in the classroom. Those of us who were habitués always said *we're going up in the canyon* or just *up the canyon*, but we were usually going through it and into the valley on the other side.

Karl had a cabin halfway up that canyon, and I took Carlos there a few times. He was with me when Karl had his little girl visiting and a rattlesnake came onto the deck. Carlos was riveted.

"I'd better kill it," Karl said.

"Kill it!" I exclaimed. "Could we throw a rock at it?"

"Because of the children," he said. "It'll come back."

"Oh dear. Couldn't we trap it? Do a relocation?" I asked. Karl was a very attractive man, and he had an unaccountable grin spread across his face. You might look at him and think he had arranged for the snake to come by and excite the guests of the day.

I had no idea that Karl had a gun or knew how to use it. Carlos and I watched, terrified for some reason, as he brought it out, leveled it at the snake, and pulled the trigger. I was sure he would miss. He was such a laid-back fun-lover, I never expected him to have mastered something like marksmanship. But that snake went limp the instant he pulled the trigger—it didn't jump or twitch, it just relaxed, if you could call death relaxed.

Carlos was fascinated. He'd found a new hero for the moment. It was the first time he'd warmed up to Karl. I tried not to show that I was appalled at killing a snake, although I'd have to admit something in me was enormously impressed with Karl too. If I wasn't with Karl, I was with Carlos that summer. I'd traded my old Scout for a red Mustang. The model had come out in April 1964 and by July I had one. It was the smartest thing any of us had ever seen. Carlos and I felt clear spritzy in it as we sped up the narrow road in our summer shirts and cutoffs. We'd go if we only had an hour, and most of it was spent driving.

After our first few ventures, we settled on a stretch of beach that was easy to get to but unfamiliar to the throngs of people who came up the canyon. It was on the south side of the reservoir so it was drenched in sunlight until almost evening. From that spot, we could swim, we could take out our rubber raft, we could fish, we could jog up and down the beach, and, of course, we could make a fire and have a picnic sitting around it—all without leaving what was essentially base camp.

Our usual trip included loading backpacks with hot dogs, potato salad, chips, olives, firewood, newspaper, matches. Occasionally we brought ketchup—never mustard. Good mustard was still an ocean away from someone in Utah. If it was warm enough, we took fishing gear. We parked beside a field, followed a trail through junegrass and wildflowers to the water's edge. We often had to make two trips. That was twenty minutes' worth of walking, ferrying equipment. It was like moving into a room in nature.

As the summer went by, we made refinements. We got so we only brought kindling and once we'd packed our gear to our spot and unloaded it, we'd shag up and down the beach looking for driftwood to burn. Eventually we learned to strip what was left of bark from the driftwood and use it for kindling. We were drawing nearer our ancestors. Always on the lookout for useful items when we were in the city, we'd found water jugs that attached to our belts and a camping table that rolled up into so many wooden slats. I don't think I spent money on anything other than outdoor equipment in those days—and Carlos. I'd gotten so I'd buy him a new shirt, a Boy Scout knife. We never did take chairs up there. We'd unroll that table, spread out our food, and drag over some stumps to sit on.

Watching Carlos start a fire was to see the craftsman in him. He'd use his bare hands to clear away the ashes from our last visit and carry them up from the beach to the grass and scatter them. "Good for thees," he'd pronounce. Then he'd crumple a few sheets of newspaper and lay them in the scooped-out pit we'd made. He would place the smallest strips of wood across the paper, crisscrossing them. Then he'd form a tepee over this with larger pieces of wood. He was attentive and careful. He could have been Prometheus bringing flame to the earth.

As the fire snapped and glowed, we got out the roasting sticks we kept tucked under some bushes, and Carlos cleaned the tips with his knife. Then he opened a particular blade and ran it around the edge of the can of olives with a lifting and pressing motion until he had that lid off. He wouldn't have anything to do with an opener once he had that knife.

We never made it very far into the afternoon before settling into the picnic everyone in America was having. It was a cross between a ceremony and a party. On the next trip up, we'd bring the same food. No one we knew abandoned hot dogs or hamburgers for *bratwurst* or *jambon royal* for another decade. Maybe they'd try an occasional sloppy joe.

The trips that sort themselves out from the other expeditions are the ones in which we took up our fishing gear. We made a great fuss of straightening it, and when the time came, we were ready to cast out a line. Carlos used a spinning rod. I wouldn't be caught dead with one, which I didn't fail to point out to him. I had my old Fenwick, and I laid out a Royal Coachman, something flashy. I don't remember ever catching a fish up there, although we'd see a few dead ones on the shore. A dead fish washed up on the beach is a great discouragement to a fisherman, but when we'd encounter one, we'd flip it into the bushes and persevere. Carlos voiced my thoughts, watching my fly float out. "Nothing! Never catch fish with thees," he said.

"It's true," I answered, laughing at his condemnation. "It's painfully true, but I like it," I told him. "There's more art to it than what I do in my studio." I'd begun to paint by then.

"Lot of talk," Carlos said. Then he chuckled. "Crazy Jeri, you not the same." He'd begun to call me by my first name by then.

"Same?" I said to him.

"My mother, my sister never do thees."

"Many women do, though. Nothing special."

"No, ver very special," he said.

"Not so bad yourself," I told him, and stopped to realize how much language he was starting to throw around and in how many attitudes. He'd always been good at bantering, but there was a new range and ease to it. Noticing that was one of the great moments of arrival for me in the journey with Carlos.

We stayed until the sun set that day, a woman and a boy—what probably looked like mother and son to the rare person riding by in a boat. I was animated, I was peaceful—we both were, and that didn't change if we brought along the French Club or Carlos's classmates. We were always boisterous in the day and hushed and mellow as the light faded, the water at first like a silver plate, then deepening to blue, to purple.

We finally put our poles down and just looked at the evening, the waves coming in, the birds swooping and dipping. "The waves make a soft sound," I said to Carlos. I could imitate it perfectly and he watched what I was doing with breath, tongue, and then tried to make the sound himself. "That's it!" I said. "It's almost a slapping sound," and I got closer to the water, leaned over, and lightly and quickly dropped my hand, palm down, on the wet sand. I remember the feeling of the slight give, the print that remained.

"By the way, some words sound just like what they describe. Slap," I said, slapping the side of my face. "The sound is almost the same."

"Slap," he said, holding onto the vowel. He did what I did—he slapped himself, saying the word. "Slap, slap—I see thees." I barely heard him murmur, "Always helping me, Jeri."

At the end of September, the leaves on the scrub oak running up the sides of the mountain began to turn red and the stands of aspen at the ridge of the meadows turned yellow, then gold. "Meybe too cold soon, meybe take picture for me next week," Carlos said to me. I brought my camera on the next trip up, and it was the last trip that season. I have a picture of him from that day. He is sitting on the end of what must have been a narrow pier that falls several feet short of the water. He's got on a shirt in various hues of blue with a bit of gold and silver—the colors of the water. His body is turned so that he's glancing over his shoulder at me. His bare legs are extended, his feet in the dirt. I could look at the expression on his face for hours at a time. He is so young, and ageless. I'd forgotten how wonderful his hair was, almost long enough to touch his eyebrows in little mussed-up tips. He looks expectant and completely comfortable in the world, and yet there is his otherworldly quality. I'm glad we had that day.

He took several pictures of me beside the fire. When I showed him the prints, he said, "Thees one. Bigger?" I liked the one he picked. There was a western woman in it—tanned, hair slightly windblown, a look of savvy contentment on her face too.

"Always remember thees," he said as we drove down Ogden Canyon.

We were buddies, we were companions. I felt like I had my brother back—the sidekick of my childhood. All my brother and I did as kids was explore nature. We never tired of finding the places moss grew under old chunks of wood, watching our footprints on the riverbank fill with water, getting close enough to a deer to see its eyelashes. My brother didn't walk until he was almost four, didn't begin to acquire language for another year. If it was limited, it was highly imaginative. "Do you want some pickaflower?" he'd say at the table, and I'd laugh and hand him the cauliflower. I'd sit with him by the hour when we were young and talk to him. I suddenly realized that I'd been saying *mamama dadada* to him almost from the time I was a baby myself. If I wasn't talking to him or hiking with him, I was combing his hair.

Carlos drew the line at anyone messing with his hair.

"Little bit too much."

IT WAS CARLOS who made a change in the pattern of our frequent Friday night taco parties. He never came on Saturday or Sunday. That was time I spent with Karl. One Friday in the fall—I remember school hadn't been in session long—Carlos and Dan had come to my house for dinner. They were best friends at school. Dan was a wonderful choice for a friend: he was sweet, he was bright, he was full of smiles. He was also spastic, and I'd noticed that Carlos took care to be around when Dan needed him.

As we were getting ready to eat, Carlos said, "Me, Dan with you?"

"You are with me," I said. "Lucky me."

"Stay with you. Nothing home," he answered.

"For tacos?" I said. "We're having tacos."

"Tacos. TV. Movie. Stay."

"Stay?" I asked.

"Like Aunt Rose. Stay night," Carlos said.

"Your mama will be lonesome if you stay," I told him. *Lonesome* took quite a while to explain and ended in an elaborate drawing of Lilly waiting and watching at the window for Carlos.

"Nothing lonesome!" he exclaimed. "Ernie, Robert, Miranda! Too many."

I knew I could call the Residence Hall and ask if it was okay for Dan to stay overnight. If you knew the parents and had their permission, you could take the residential students from the dorm at will. It was considered a good thing, and rightly so, to have them in homes as much as possible. Carlos brought the phone to me and wrote down his number. I had it memorized by then, but I took the paper in my hand and dialed Lilly. I felt like I already had so much of Carlos, and I hesitated. Carlos was chirping in the background, "Stay."

"Oh sure, he can stay," Lilly said, as she almost always did. "That's good for him. He goes crazy with Ernie here. Those two are always fighting."

"Shall I come get some things for him?"

"What does he need?" she asked.

"Pajamas, a toothbrush?"

"He don't care. You got an old shirt?" The next seven words were said so fast I could hardly understand them. "He likes to sleep in my shirts."

I made the call to the Residence Hall, nodding to the boys as permission was given. Dan did a dance of pure joy. I called it the Rabbit Hash Dance, reviving an old line I'd picked up somewhere, or made up—I've lost track.

It wasn't long before my two little monkeys were romping through the house in white T-shirts. By the time I said, "It's ten o'clock—it's time for bed," they were deep into their whooping Cowboys and Indians.

"No, eleven better," Carlos said. He could implore for all the world. It was the one mode that wasn't effective with me.

"No. Ten is better," I said, and I tucked them both into my double bed and made a place for myself on the couch.

Carlos began to come to some of my school events that year. He came to a French Club party, and he managed to turn it into all but an international exchange. I hadn't set out to have the occasion carry its lesson, but it did. What a deaf boy inadvertently taught foreign language students was immeasurable.

We gathered in one end of the gym. The first thing at any of those events was to get out the Edith Piaf records and listen to them as we arranged the chairs and a makeshift kitchen. Then we got out the one Isabelle Aubret recording we had. I'd personally brought it back from Paris; it was a very hot item. We'd always sit around and wail with her: *"Et maintenant, que vais-je fair—e? Maintenant que tu es part—ie."* We'd laugh at ourselves sobbing out the song. Carlos laughed at us too, then conducted the last chorus in lachrymose fashion. Drew led us in the playful *Coucou Hibou*, heads bobbing, spirits blithe. By the time we got to *"dans la forêt lointaine, on entend le coucou,"* we'd shifted into variations and harmony, even rounds. There were some good singers in that group; I was not one of them, but I recognized a fine rendition when I heard it, and Carlos seemed to as well.

Then we got out the crêpe pan. It didn't get pressed into service for anything else—it sat in my office, waiting for the next party. On this occasion, my students showed Carlos how to do the last-minute crêpe flip.

I looked over to where he was, later in the evening, and saw him sitting in the middle of a circle of students who were teaching him to say *bonjour*, a million gestures going into the endeavor. They taught him just as I had taught them, putting their index finger beside their noses to show him how to feel the nasal quality in *bon*, and then floating their hands through the air to show him the glide of *jour*. Carlos knew the gestures. I sat there smiling, something wonderful coming together and I was there to witness it—to have set it in motion, actually. In three tries Carlos was clipping off the *bon* and sliding into *jour* like a Frenchman. He didn't fail to add a little Gallic eyebrow. I can't remember if we saw a film that night. We probably danced—everyone was a dancing fool in that era, and that called for switching to the Beatles. Whatever we did made us laugh. The half-English, half-French conversations—*J'ai faim*, *mais* I don't want *la même* damn *chose*, Carlos teaching my students to say *adios*, goodbye *amigo*. I'd never heard him speak a Spanish word, and I was—we all were—enchanted.

Carlos joined my senior English class to see a Shakespearean production of *Macbeth*. I wondered if he would be bored blind, but I'd forgotten how much action there is in it. Someone is always leading an army or drawing a dagger or gesturing to a ghost or washing blood from tormented hands. I'd told Carlos a little bit about Shakespeare, and he'd listened—he could see it mattered to me. "He is very good. Maybe the best in the world," I told him.

"Where live?" Carlos asked.

"He lived in England over four hundred years ago. Almost everybody still thinks he is the best."

"Dead how long?"

"He died in 1616, a very easy number to remember."

"The best," he pondered. Something in me thrilled at introducing those two—the supreme handler of language and the deaf boy with his own fanciful gifts and sense of drama, a boy who might have written plays. I tried to imagine seeing *Macbeth* without hearing it, and the lines that came back to me made me momentarily sad.

> And all our yesterdays have lighted fools
> The way to dusty death.

Carlos would have loved the images, the language: a dagger of the mind; full of scorpions is my mind.

He watched the play intently. "Not friendly," he said as the final curtain fell in a great swoosh. Everyone around him burst out laughing.

"Did you like it?" I had tried to keep myself from asking that.

"Little bit," he said. I couldn't gauge to what degree politeness affected his answer. "Thees woman," he went on, "what's the *matter* with her?" He was still thinking about the play that had thundered across the stage as we left the exotic and colorful Peery's Egyptian Theater.

"Little bit mixed up," he said. "Little bit silly."

"The clothes?" I asked him.

"Know thees. From movies," he said. "Little bit too much."

Carlos visited all my classes that year, including the Sunday School class I sometimes taught. The first one he came to was my junior English class—the accelerated section of straight-A students. He stood at the front of the room like an ambassador. The exchange was simple and something in it was profound.

"What is your name?" Marianne asked him. She was in the front row, shy and brilliant. I would see her forty years later and she would ask, "What happened to Carlos?"

"My dame is Carlos Louis Salazar," he said, having trouble with the *n*, his voice ascending as always with *Louis Salazar*. The students melted. For once they didn't want to laugh.

"Where do you live?" Polly asked. She had enough pizzazz for the entire student body, and she gave him that ready, almost daring smile I still remember.

"I live at 183 Patterson Avenue," he said. I always want to say he chirped because his voice was so birdlike, high and melodic and repetitive in its patterns.

"What do you like to do?" Tom asked. He would become Dr. Rosenberg and put part of me back together after too many ski crashes, a lot of them with him.

Carlos looked at me. "Watch," I said quietly. He turned back to Tom, and Tom repeated the question, slowing it.

"Like?" he said. I could see the minute he understood *like* by the way he cocked his head.

He looked at me again. "Like to do," I said, breaking with my preference not to shorten or distort a sentence with Carlos.

"What I like do?" he asked. "Like to come your class." He was a skillful ambassador, and clever. Everyone in the room beamed.

"How old are you?" Drew asked. He was chuckling. He was enjoying Carlos.

"I will be eleven in November." The syllables couldn't have been more even if they'd been tapped out to a metronome, probably Lilly's influence. He counted on his fingers. "Three months. Then two years 'til teenager." I could see no one had understood *teenager*. I tried to stay quiet.

"Almost what?" Drew asked, not the least uncomfortable.

"Eleven. Twelve. Thirteen," he said, his voice going high on *thirteen*. "Almost teen." The students all but applauded. "How old are *you*?" Carlos asked Drew. "What's *your* name?"

He could focus something—it wasn't exactly how simplistic the questions were; it was more than that.

Drew wasn't catching any subtleties. He was lost in delight. "I'm seventeen and my name is Drew Ellington. Thanks for asking."

"Will you come back and see us again?" Marianne asked him.

"I like thees," he said. I was afraid he was going to bow, but he had an impeccable sense of what you do and what you don't do. He was charming beyond description. I don't know if he'd ever had occasion to stand before a hearing group of people. You would have thought he'd rehearsed for months.

My students worked harder after that, assessed what they had, aimed higher.

"Has he had his birthday yet?" they asked in November, and several of them brought cookies for me to deliver to him.

When winter came and my students planned their annual caroling bash, they said, "You'll bring Carlos, won't you?" I was proud of them on that outing; they were good at communicating with Carlos, and when we were back in the classroom, I asked them what they'd learned about language.

"It's made of a lot of small pieces," one of the boys said. "I didn't realize how complex it is." And I knew that part of what he was saying was *I didn't realize how lucky I am. I don't even remember trying to learn to talk.*

"Could he be our Christmas family? Could we bring things for him?" they asked in December.

They were so bountiful in their outpouring of gifts for the Salazars on Patterson Avenue, it was uncomfortable. It took three cars to deliver what they'd brought, including rolls of carpeting. I was amazed, and dismayed. How could I say to them, *This is not the best way.* I wish I *had* said that. I was learning myself about giving. Even Carlos quipped, "Too much!" and went up the street and disappeared with his buddies when the delivery was made.

I said to my students later, "What do you think about our trip to the Salazars?"

"We embarrassed them," one of the girls said, one of the quieter ones. "Did we make them feel poor?"

"We did," Polly said. "And the neighbors were watching."

A show of riches, I was thinking to myself. It was a parade of excess.

"Maybe it's best not to bring someone too much of what he doesn't have," I said. "What would you want if you didn't have much?"

"I'd want what I *want,*" Marianne said, "not what I need."

Beautiful, beautiful moments in the classroom, Carlos woven into them, taking us all to thoughts about language and where it led us in fitting, in belonging, in accepting.

"No."

MANY MONTHS PASSED before I saw Carlos compromised. *Compromised* isn't the right word. *Broken* is. Everyone's role in it is illuminating—it plays in my mind like a movie.

It is April 1966. The white tulips are up in my yard, and daffodils encircle the buildings at Carlos's school. It looks just as it did when I met him two years before. On this Friday the boys are returning from the restroom as I walk into Marian's class. I'm there early and the students have started to leave. The feeling in the room startles me. Some major shift has occurred. I hear the surreptitious, exclusive laughter and squeals, see the almost hysterical movements of the boys, notice the freewheeling patterns of wetness across their pants and shirts, and most of all gauge the disgust of the girls. I don't have any idea what has just taken place, but I feel myself pull back from the scene. I don't want to know what happened, and I don't ask any questions. Rooms full of tension are rooms I always want to leave. The Carlos in this room is unfamiliar to me. He's the cock of the walk and when he sees me, he turns away, but not before I see something entreating in his eyes.

The scene plays out. "He's on one today," Marian is saying. "He's been in the bushes with the girls, showing them their proper positions." Her voice is full of disgust. She is slamming around, arranging school supplies as she talks. "I guess you can see he's been decorating them in the bathroom. That would be a delicate way to put it." She can't know what transpired in there, I think to myself. I take a long look at Carlos. He is accustomed to the role of instigator, but I understand that something more is going on with him now. Marian is still throwing words around. "After a lifetime of standing by him! Villain! This is the last year I'll have him!"

"I'd better be going . . ." I begin to say.

"You're not going," she tells me. I don't dream of countermanding her. She looks at me, and I sense how shattered she is, how deep in the furious current of disappointment. I can see that more clearly now than I could then.

I wait. I am becoming aware of my stake in the status quo. "Don't worry," she is saying. "It is the style you love in him, if not the virtue. It started with a robbery at lunchtime." She turns to him and cries out "Robber!" When she says the word *robber*, I have to suppress the well-rehearsed instinct to laugh when something is sufficiently inappropriate. But I can tell that Carlos picked up the word, and I feel deep alarm. This isn't a scene he should witness, and I realize he's far more than a witness. At some level I am angry at her display of anger.

"Marian . . ." I start to say, but I know I don't have a card in the world to play. "He marched in here," she continues. She is terrifically unwinning, her face hard, her hair seeming to fly about. "And he got into my purse and took out a twenty-dollar bill." She turns to him again. "Foul!" she hurls. "Ignominious! Obstreperous!" I'm grateful Carlos doesn't know what she is saying, and I'm sure she wouldn't have talked this way if she thought he did, but a frog wouldn't have missed the tone. He looks like he's been hit, and he leaves so quietly I ache.

"He marched straight down to the office and cashed the twenty for a ten and ten ones." I'm trying to keep on top of this. I assume this is speculation. "There was a substitute in the office who was stupid enough to do it for him." I'm having a hard time listening to her, and I have to force myself not to go after Carlos.

She charges through the rest of the story—the money passed out among the students while her back was turned, their irrepressible delight greater than their fear.

She is getting tired now and her voice drops. "After a while I began to see them tuck something into pockets, check to see that it was still there, fuss with purses. Fingers were flashing messages to one another in what they thought were unobserved signals. So I began to examine."

"You didn't find anything," I say.

"Oh I did," she answers. "I found ten dollars in ones scattered among them."

I think she is going to cry, and that scares me more than anything else that has happened. She is large and solid and intimidating.

"Someone else took it," I say. "You didn't find any money on him."

And then Carlos comes back into the room.

"No," she says, " but I'm about to. I plan to give him a shakedown he'll never forget. In fact, why don't *you* do it?" I've never seen her this vitriolic. "It's time you see what you're dealing with," she adds.

I don't miss the anger spilling in my direction. I reach for my car keys. "I would never search him," I say. It sounds different than I mean it, sounds sanctimonious. Then I look at Carlos, I see his face. He's frightened, really frightened. This is his calm Miss Bentley. "I'll ask him if he has the money, and he'll tell me." That sounds different than I want it to as well, and I make it worse. "Let's not violate his character."

"Character is key there," she hurls back. "Expose his fraudulence, that's what you'll do." I begin to see that she is making this as jarring as she can for him, for his sake.

I turn away from her and ask Carlos, "Do you have any of the money Miss Bentley is looking for? Some of the boys and girls had some dollar bills." Even as I ask him, I can't believe I've allowed myself to be drawn into this. I can see that he understands. He looks at me with his brown eyes all surprise and slow sorrow. He is stunned that I think he has any of it, and again I haven't conveyed what I mean. I mean to establish his innocence. I am so sorry I have asked him this, I have to battle tears myself. I must be his steady friend here, and I see that I would hate to be the one who disappoints.

"No," he says, his voice suddenly low and soft. Heartbreak and despair threaten every syllable of the next words. "Never, never." All his loyalty to the part of his life Marian and I represent is unveiled, and I feel strung along it like a criminal myself.

"Never, never my foot!" Marian is saying, and for the first time I really feel like turning and decking her, or slapping her the way they do in movies to get someone out of their hysteria. But she goes on. "Let's just start with *this!*" She takes his glasses case from his shirt pocket. It moves into slow motion for me. I can't even look at Carlos.

Suddenly Marian is waving a ten-dollar bill in his face and saying, "No, never! That's what you're made of!" He has shattered her hopes for him, I finally see that clearly, and she can only stand there and rave.

But my pity and my attention are all on Carlos, whose worlds are colliding. What I am fumbling with is not the fact of the money he has taken and lied about, but the urgency with which he has told the version he must somehow make true. Before many more years go by, I will understand that his urgency is always for what he *wants* to be the truth. I think I would rather relive any moment with Carlos than the one in which I see a young boy confront the split in himself, a split driven deep into him by the many spheres that shaped and claimed him. I had a part in that.

His entire body turns to sadness. And when the emotion spills down his face in tears, he steps back and walks out of the room. I stand in the hallway and watch him until he is outside, running by then. I follow to the outer door of the school and see him run with fury and wild despair. He flees across the grass and out into the field that borders the School for the Deaf, covering it in the course of a few seconds as he hurls himself away from his shame and heartbreak, black hair flying up into the wind he creates, arms pumping terribly to carry him from the looks he must see on our faces.

I watch him race across that field and away from whatever tied him to me. I see it often, and I'm always certain as I stare after him that I will never see him again. Finally he disappears into the foothills above the school.

I was cold all the way through by then, and I turned to find Marian beside me. We walked to our cars in silence, and I went home.

Everything was falling away from him—I could see it as it happened. It was all I could see.

"I don't care."

IT WENT LIKE THAT. The lark days of knowing Carlos were gone in a few hours. I would almost never again not feel anxiety about him. I did manage to learn not to have that anxiety dictate my response. The conundrum was in place—no solution to the problem, a paradox.

Seeing him run into the foothills, being with him that disrupting afternoon, wasn't just a heartache, and it was far beyond a wake-up call. You couldn't get around all of it with one word, but if I had only one, it would be *marginalize,* perhaps for both of us. I was seeing a few worlds collide myself—my wanting a son; my loving this boy differently than you love a son—loving him for his jazz, his theater, his tossing the world off, his uniqueness, his seeing in me what many people missed—and yes, his beauty, his comely, endearing ways. And my loving the danger in him, his control over incidents and personalities so immense he seemed to have concluded that he could control even the truth.

I could see the division that pointed to the worlds that claimed him—his street and his street smarts, his friends there that were getting old enough to be on the wrong side of the law, his efforts to enter a vastly different life at school where trouble invariably found him. And then there was his friendship with a woman as wild-hearted as he was, someone who wished the golden apples of the sun for him, someone fourteen years older.

I was in it for the long haul, I knew that, or thought I did. But there was a new component. I was very carefully examining what I could add and what I could take away. I sat at my table for a long time the evening Carlos ran into the foothills. I'd made it from a slice of burled pine, a very thick slice, and I ran my hand along the heavy grain and traced out knots. I didn't want things to change. I wanted a house full of deaf boys to tear around on Friday nights and eat a hundred tacos. I wanted Carlos to stay a boy—I hadn't had him long enough. I'd just begun to bake the right amount of cupcakes. And somewhere in there, I wanted not to neglect Karl—the man in my life who wasn't quite the right man. Nothing told me that more than my letting everything revolve around Carlos.

I got up and opened the refrigerator. I closed it. I had a parrot, Eugene, who spent a lot of time on the refrigerator, which didn't do much for the contents inside. "Blue," I said to him. "Blue, blue, blue," he said back. He was another language study.

I made myself a cup of tea and sat back down at the table and cradled the hot mug in my hands. I watched the light fade. I could still see Carlos running. I'd never seen anyone run in full desperation before, with the pure intent to escape. I shivered and drank my tea. I looked at my watch. It had been two hours and Carlos had no jacket. April nights could be very cold in the foothills of the Wasatch. I went out onto the deck and stood looking up at them. Purple shadows cut across patches of snow. You rarely saw the green of the trees; they were just far enough away to lose their local color.

I thought again of the early trappers and explorers up in those mountains. Miles Goodyear had had the sense to come down into the valley, a delta between the city's two rivers, and establish his Fort Buenaventura. It's a tourist attraction now, not a mile from the street Carlos lived on.

The phone rang, and I stepped back inside and picked it up.

"He deserved it," Marian said. There was no hello.

"No," I said. "No one deserves his hand."

"You're right for once," she said. "Will you go to Lilly's? You know that's hard for me."

As soon as I was in the car, I thought again of the role I was playing in Carlos's life. "To marginalize," I said aloud. I estimated the effects on him of differing economic systems, value systems, educational levels, social positions—social tiers, really. As I drove along Twenty-sixth Street, the houses got smaller, the yards less groomed. I crossed the downtown area, limited and beginning to deteriorate, and passed on through the industrial district, even more limited. I turned south on Wall Street and drove through the warehouses and car lots to his street. It hadn't changed much. I tried to imagine what it would be for him to step from a warm car with a nice coat and new shoes onto Patterson Avenue as I walked through the boys and girls, cousins, friends, standing in twos and threes along the picket fence. They were quiet now. I felt their eyes on me as Carlos must have when he came back in new clothes, new shoes. And I saw in my mind how he must re-enter this world, saw him toss the coat on the floor in a corner, unbutton his shirt, unbutton the sleeves and push them up, run a hand through his hair, leaving it messy. He'd have to somehow make himself acceptable in his own home.

Lilly came to the door. I stood there on the porch. The first thing I noticed was my photograph on a bookshelf. Later Lilly would tell me, "He don't let nobody touch that."

"Carlos ran away," I began. My voice wasn't steady, and I couldn't continue.

"He told me that." She said it more quickly than anything I'd ever heard her say.

"Is he home?" I asked, incredulous. I had envisioned him staying out in the foothills for a week or two, long enough to have to trap and roast a rabbit, come back disheveled, chilled. I reminded myself it wasn't a Dickens tale here, but it more or less was. And I remembered a line in a book I'd read about native Indian people and the white people who asked two questions, "Are they dirty? Do they steal?"

"Is he here?" I repeated.

"Yeah, he's here," she said. "He don't want to be bothered." She looked down and made a little sound. She was uncomfortable telling me this.

"I understand," I said. "I wanted to be sure he was okay, and I'll tell Marian."

"That's nice of you," she said, looking back up at me. And she added, "We were so poor." I took it as an explanation.

On the drive home, I thought how much trouble was involved in taking a child from his home, his street, putting him in a classroom and making something different of him. Aspects of it could seem like abuse to a child who was deaf.

"I don't care!" was Carlos's answer to the hard press of his early school years. It was more a shield than an attitude, but he could fool you. There was real intensity there. "I don't care!" was one of the first phrases he'd learned, and he could utter it a hundred ways to explain his response to difficulty, to pain, to torment, to confusion, to loss, to sorrow. Only those who came to know him deeply became aware of the fine and fragile thing, a butterfly beneath bravado, behind his "I don't care!"

I saw Carlos downtown later that week. He was wearing glasses, and they changed him so much I wasn't sure it was him. He had on an old navy pea coat big enough for a man, and as he turned, I saw the sign he'd pinned on the back. There was suddenly no mistaking him, although he looked too small. He'd drawn a picture on the sign. In it he stood facing forward with his hand raised, almost like a traffic cop, signing. Above the figure was the word *Deaf* and below it, *Carlos.* So he'd put the visual between him and an uncomfortable encounter. But why now? To set himself apart before anyone could accidentally discover the news about him? Was there more than just self-protection in it? He had begun to draw almost daily, and I knew he had to be reaching for every dimension of communication available to him. He probably found focus and release in drawing. For whatever reasons, he was making a record of his life through his amazing sketches.

He saw me at the intersection, and I waved. It was probably a wan, pathetic gesture. I thought I saw him mouth "I don't care!" and he turned and ran, black hair splitting the wind, and everything was falling away from him again, this time including me.

DeaF
Carlos

PART TWO

"Do everything one more time."

I LEFT UTAH not too long after that. Looking back, the decision seems composed of equal parts courage and cowardice. I must have felt it was a good thing for Carlos as well as for me. I knew it was for Karl, or thought I did. In those days I adhered to the notion that it was better to move on if you weren't going to marry the man you were spending your time with. I did it literally. My sojourn in Montreal provided a way for us to go our separate ways. It was meant to be merciful. I later concluded that no break is merciful.

A handful of months went by before I packed my necessaries and drove north and then east. Those months were full of Carlos, although I hadn't expected them to be. I'd hardly seen him since his *I don't care* flurry. He would storm into adolescence now, I told myself—you've had your moment upon his stage. There will be more, but not for a while. That part was wrong as well.

Carlos swept up to me a few months after I'd seen him downtown and only a few weeks after I had accepted a position teaching the deaf in Montreal. He trotted out his old line, "Home. With." He wasn't as cavalier, I noticed that.

We fell right back into palling around, but now I made a more conscious effort to use the time on his behalf. I got so I arranged outings that would take him into the territory of new language. He was to a point of quickness and responsiveness that made it enthralling. Words combined into concepts almost before the eye—it was as though you were seeing a brain, or rather a whole personality, develop in one of those time-lapse photography wonders.

Another area I reluctantly and very carefully ventured into was his uneven behavior. He had two responses to the world now. I had to deal with my concern that I was part of the shift—had skewed what could have been a more consistent environment. Whatever the causes, he kept the courtliness and charm that had been so winning when I'd first met him, but there was a new element of mockery in him. If he denigrated someone, and oh, he could do it, I reminded him that that other person was worthy of his consideration. "He's as good as you," I said to him when he made no end of fun of his friend Dan one night at my home. "He's your brother."

"Brother!" he cried out. "Not my brother. Ernie's my brother. Robert's my brother." I don't think Edwin had come along yet.

There was a boy in his class who stumbled. He actually stumbled in every way. He could trip over nothing, and his hair would sweep down and his glasses would drop almost off his nose. He stumbled even worse in class, unable either to sign or speak with any dexterity. When others went to the board to do math problems and returned to their seats, he would linger, staring. You could sense the blankness of the stare even from his back. Finally the teacher would lead him to his seat.

The imitation Carlos did of this boy was precise in every detail. It was excruciating to see, and even though its unsparing nature caused you pain, you could hardly keep from laughing—it was an uncomfortable reminder that imitation is almost always done of someone you consider less. It's the nature of satire, and it was Carlos's specialty. He would shrink his head down into his neck, sag his pants around his ankles, nudge his glasses still further down his nose, sniffle, and take on a quantum of befuddlement. It was uncanny. He *became* that boy. His classmates howled at this. Then he went one step too far. That part of it I've put out of my mind.

"He's your brother, too," I said to him.

"I'm not stupid!" he replied. This was closer to a bark than the chirp I'd come to anticipate. It took me by surprise, but I continued. "If you stepped way back," I said, "if you went far from the earth and glanced back, he'd look like a brother to you." I think that's a pretty crazy answer to have given him. He did too, and he communicated it.

"We're all the same," I said, trying again. "We're equals. Equal value." I cut up pieces of paper and wrote names on them: Dan, Ricky, Dewayne, Carlos. I made them all the same size. "They're equal," I said. "No one is first."

"Numba one?" he said. He'd heard the expression, and his rendition took it to a parody.

"Right," I answered. "No number ones."

"Oh sure," I thought I heard him say. I could see he regretted it, and he grew quiet. Later that week he came by my house on a bike, sat down beside me with no preamble, and said, "Everybody okay?"

"That's it!" I said. "Everybody is okay."

Still later he came back with a picture he'd drawn of a big house and a boy on a bike. He sat down beside me again, and on the other half of the page, he drew a boy lying in the rain far from a very small house, no more than a triangle on the distant horizon.

"Same?" he asked.

"Equal," I said. "Not the same."

He was a boy struggling with unequal opportunity, deafness, and probably smallness. Everyone was growing around him. He hadn't changed.

When I told Carlos I was going to Montreal to teach the deaf, he looked at me in bewilderment. I got out a map and showed him where it was. "How long drive?" he asked, holding an imaginary steering wheel, a big one.

"Six days if you stop often, like me," I told him. He flew to his desk, flew back to take another look at the atlas. Then he fell to drawing.

"How soon?" he asked the next time I saw him. He could tell I didn't understand. "How soon Montreal?" The added word came out close to the French: *Mon-réal.* He never got a *t* in it.

"I'll go when the next school year begins," I told him. "At the end of the summer."

"Do everything one more time," he said. And we did. We got out the old rubber raft and took all his friends to Pineview Reservoir. We went to the rodeo at the old fairgrounds beside the river. We wore our cowboy boots and swaggered to the concession stand for hot dogs. We watched *Mission: Impossible*, the kind of television show he loved. There was so much action in it, language was almost an aside. We saw the Fourth of July parade and stepped up to pet ponies that were slowed by the big floats ahead of them. We had endless barbeques, rallied teams of his friends for work on community projects. We visited museums, air shows, anything that could capture his fancy and provide him with a chance to add to his language.

I nearly got him killed several times. We went skiing in the last of the snow in mid-July, hiking to get to it. I was crazy about the sport—it was my sublime endeavor. I would have hiked two hours to ski five minutes, and I tended to underestimate how difficult the trip down was going to be. Carlos had been with me on a beginner hill and had shown such promise and such relish for skiing that I took him along.

"Think of flying and stay behind me," I'd said to him. Crazy, crazy advice to give Carlos Louis Salazar. My heart stopped when halfway down his first run, his scarf—which had fluttered out behind him like a blue-and-white flag—went down and didn't come up. He had on a light-colored parka and pants so the main thing I could see of him was that scarf I'd brought him from Austria. When it dropped from sight, I could scarcely breathe. Of course, I'd said go slow, and I had gotten out in front of him and tried to show him how to traverse the mountain. It was only moments before he headed straight down, gaining speed on the steep and icy incline, my cries of *Fall down! Fall down!* having no chance to reach him. What had I been thinking to let him get out ahead of me like that?

By the time I got to him, a few other skiers as crazy as we were had gathered. Carlos lay crumpled in the center of them. He stayed down long enough for us to begin improvising a sled to take him out. I couldn't let myself think that he was unconscious, although he appeared to be when I first knelt at his side. By the time we'd lashed a roll of plastic and some rope together, he had sat straight up, gotten to his feet, looked at our creation, and set off again, my protests echoing as his scarf flew out.

On our last trip to the reservoir before I left, he dropped out of the boat. I'd seen him lean over, gaze, seem to hover between the boat and the water before the splash. I went overboard almost at the same instant, groping madly before he disappeared in the dark water beyond the reach of my hands and eyes.

A time or two he'd been angry enough at me to kill me. He wasn't as accommodating as he once had been. When I'd refused to let him walk the pipeline that ran two hundred feet above the Ogden Canyon highway, his open, engaging manner crumbled and there, where the eyes had shown with eagerness, were eyes suddenly smaller and hardened to a dull glaze. His full mouth thinned to a threatening line, and the delicate wings of his nostrils whitened. Almost simultaneously, the lightness and deftness of his movements dried into plodding, and everything in him announced *no* to me. Since he had few guises, or skills, for handling anger, it was always a raw thing to see.

His possessiveness was becoming equally developed, perhaps because I was leaving. "A child lands in a relationship like a torpedo," I told Marian one afternoon when we'd gone for tea. "How does everything else . . . you wonder how a marriage survives it."

"Do you know any that have?" she said. "I don't imagine your lawyer likes sharing you. Heaven knows it has required generosity on his part."

"They do cut a wide swath around each other, don't they?" I said. "Carlos is better at letting me juggle it all than Karl is. Not that he isn't always a gentleman, but at heart he doesn't enjoy Carlos much more than he would a head-on collision with a bear."

"He's hit something a trifle harder to walk away from, he knows that. You do too, don't you? Carlos can dance circles around Karl for pure style. How did you fall in with someone so predictable?"

"Beguiled," I said. "By a beautiful mouth. Unflawed chemistry."

"Unflawed?" She looked up. I wished I weren't having this conversation.

"Take your body where you want, the soul will find its home," she continued. "And that's what makes the two of them—shall we say at odds?" She'd ordered fruit with her tea—actually she was having hot chocolate and I was having tea—and she organized the pieces of cantaloupe and watermelon as we talked. "A lot of women have traded an average husband for an excellent son, my dear."

"I don't like to think it's that serious," I said. We were near a window that provided a beautiful view of the mountains. Outside the sun was blazing. My eyes wandered up toward the foothills where Carlos had made his flight more than two years earlier. The soft green that I loved in Utah had begun to fade at the lower elevations. "The mountains are leaving their velvet," I said to Marian.

"What does that mean? Is that some of your moose lore?"

"Yes—moose—when their horns are in their velvet, they look like—like velvet. Then they shed them."

I looked at the mountains awhile then turned toward Marian and said, "Karl calls Carlos 'Wonder Boy' and Carlos calls him 'Animal.'"

Marian laughed with pleasure. As though she guessed I was remembering her last encounter with him, she said, "Any attorney worth his scales of justice should be able to define 'jurisprudence.' Remind me to give him another quiz when I see him."

"You're hard on him," I said, surprising myself. "I am too, that's the trouble."

"Well, be grateful for what's what," she said. Then she began to laugh again. "'Animal' is too wonderful even for Carlos to come up with. It's precise. Maybe just a trace of Oedipal jealousy in the Garden?" Then she stopped laughing and said quietly, "Remember, Carlos is the focus, not the cause."

As it turned out, Karl and I both had unlucky crashes. I survived my crash. Karl was burned to death in a plane that went down on a flight back from Mexico. It was in the middle of Carlos's struggle for his own life, but that was still a decade away.

"Sons," I said. "I was going to name my boy James Christian, James after my husband. Actually I don't even know if it was a boy. I asked but I wasn't told."

"That was the drunk driver accident, wasn't it?" Marian said, her voice full of an unusual amount of feeling. I looked down at my hands, and I saw that they had aged and I hadn't noticed. "Let's go find Wonder Boy," I said, looking up.

Surely having a son wouldn't be like this, I told myself, delight splintered by silly vying, and for what? Did begetting one kind of love have to diminish another? And the shackling—the being bounded by the circumference of Karl's generosity of spirit. I must have known another limitation was possible too—the one imposed by Carlos's excess of spirit.

"I'm going to Montreal," I told Karl at the end of July.

"For a visit?" he asked.

"For the winter."

"North for the winter? Isn't that the wrong direction?" The note of dismissal was a new one for him.

"Beautiful small little house."

CARLOS AND I drove to Idaho to visit my family on a whim a few weeks before I left Utah. My father was inhospitable to Carlos, and we left after lunch. I wondered why I'd thought my father could handle a deaf Spanish-American boy. I was mad at myself, and I suggested the thing that would comfort me. "Let's go on up to the old sawmill cabin," I said to him. "Do you know what a cabin is?"

"Cabin?" he repeated.

"I'll show you a cabin," I told him. "It's a little home in the mountains." We went to the co-op on the way out of Pocatello and rounded up warmer clothes and kept driving north. I was the only one who went up to that cabin then, but I went often enough to keep it clean. People had begun to break in and take things. I never could have predicted what they would take. They left the bronze horses on the mantle and took the water heater. I didn't miss it—there was no water connection in place anyway. We drove past little farm towns—Firth, Shelley, Ririe. They were scattered among potato and alfalfa fields. I liked the rotation of the green and gold in the farmland, the tractors and irrigation equipment and old trucks in silhouette against the late sun.

We left the highway in Rexburg and drove through Main Street. It was pure Western small town—the faded marquee of the Romance Theater, the old Madison High School, the Classique Dress Shop, the Joy Drugstore with a Rexall sign in the window, Broulim's grocery store. You didn't have to leave Main Street for what you needed.

"I was born here," I told Carlos. I thought of my witty, straightforward grandmother, whose winter home had been just a few blocks from

Main. She was my favorite person on earth, and when she left the earth, she didn't lose her standing. I looked out the car window and remembered her telling me what had happened in front of the Classique. "That's where I ran into Sarah," she had said. "She stepped up and asked me how I liked my new daughter-in-law. I don't, I told her. She's too clean for me." She'd laughed when she told me that story, laughed at her own cheekiness and at how wrong she'd been. "You don't figure at first what you'll figure in a few months," she had added, and I took notice.

"You busy remembering," Carlos said.

"Yes, yeah, yes." I was wondering why I'd chosen to leave the West and all that was familiar to me. "Let's stop for some groceries and get up in those mountains in time to fix dinner," I said to Carlos.

When we got to Ashton, I turned to him so he could see me clearly and said, "In ten minutes we'll be in forest. Do you know this word—forest?"

"Trees," he said.

"Yes, see way ahead, the hillside is dark. Wow, we'll just drive right into trees."

"Into trees," he said.

"Pine trees. They can be five thousand years old." I turned so he could see me. "They can grow right out of rock. I'll show you. If you roll the window down, you'll smell them." And then there we were, in the forest of my childhood, Carlos by my side. I remembered what it was for me at his age—at thirteen.

Carlos rolled his window down halfway. "I smell thees," he said. "Different than Utah trees." I had noticed that the Idaho forest smelled different—it was richer, spicier, more layered. Maybe it was the variety of trees—lodgepole pine and Douglas fir and limber pine and whitebark pine and blue spruce and, once in a while, aspen.

"There are trees like this from here to Alaska," I told him. He knew a lot about Alaska—his classmate Dewayne was from there.

"Alaska," he said.

"How does it smell to you?" I asked him.

"Warm. Nice. Like big greenhouse." I liked his description. It accounted for the intimate feeling of a forest with its own ecosystem—its humidity, its variety of plant and animal life. I watched as the landmarks I loved went by: Pond's Lodge; Gordon's Elk Creek station, looking remodeled; McCrea's Bridge, looking a little worn; and then the fork west toward Yale Creek.

I could barely drive and keep turning toward him, but I was so interested in his response, I managed. "We will live like little, contented animals for a day. We'll have to go scampering for wood and scampering for water. Now watch right up ahead—we'll go around this corner and up this hill," and I pointed to the open meadow on my right. "See that little cabin? We'll stay there. That's where I spent all my summers as a child."

"We'll stay there," he said, and I had my brother back, my son, and I showed him the best of my life. We stepped out of the car and just breathed.

"Happy Jeri," he said.

"I'm happy to have you here." I reached over and tousled his hair. Then I found the key tucked behind a rafter that I could just reach. I opened that old screen door, put the skeleton key in the lock, and we walked into the back porch—what we always called the back porch, but it was more than a porch. You could see the enameled wood-burning stove in the kitchen and beyond that the fireplace in the living room.

"Beautiful little small house," Carlos said.

"Beautiful boy in my mountain home. We call this kind of house a cabin." I could see him wonder why I called him *beautiful boy*.

"Cabin," he said. "Nothing scared?"

"Nothing scared," I answered. "Never ever." We went back to the car and brought in our bags. I showed him his little room off the screened porch. The first thing he did was climb up on the high, quilt-covered bed, and look out the window that opened onto the porch because it had been added on. He thought it was the funniest thing he'd ever seen to have a window not look outside.

"I'll show you how to live in the forest." We went into the kitchen and I found what we called the lifter on top of the stove and fitted it into the circular lid that covered the fire box. I lifted it off and said, "Will you make a fire in there—just the same way as we do on the beach?" I reached for the newspaper that we kept way too close to the stove, and he crumpled it and put it into the fire box. "Never saw thees," he said. Then we went out to the woodshed and brought in firewood of various sizes.

"Too big," he said. I took him back out into the forest and we gathered up dried branches and twigs that had fallen on the forest floor. If they were too long, we stood them against a tree and put a foot to them before we took our collection inside. "This is perfect kindling. Wait 'til you hear how it burns."

"Nothing hear," he said, just as I realized it.

"You *get* everything though," I told him.

He placed the kindling into the stove and struck the match I handed him. He held it to the paper and stood there watching the small fire. Then he replaced the lid with such care I wished my grandmother could see him warming himself before her enameled stove with the soft green trim.

"Need more wood," he said, and I took him up to the woodshed and lay firewood across his extended arms like my grandfather had done with me. "Enough," he said, and I grabbed a few pieces and we went back to the kitchen with them. It was already beginning to warm. Then we went out onto the porch and each got a bucket.

"Come with me," I said, and we walked on the barely visible path to the cookhouse. The lupine and fleabane and larkspur were still up. And the sticky geraniums—they lasted through everything. "We'll get water up there," I said, pointing to where the cookhouse had been. "See the red-handled deal standing out there? That's the handle of a pump. There used to be a big cabin with a dining room right beside the pump."

"Pump?" he asked. "Funny word."

"I always thought so, but a pump is one cool piece of business."

"Cool piece of business," he repeated. I could see him thinking over that combination of words. When we got to it, he said, "Thees very poor living, Jeri. Far long from water."

"You won't think this is poor living in one hour," I told him. "This is the best it gets." I took hold of the red handle and made the quick pumping motion that primes the mechanism, and then I did the long, measured presses until a little water and then a stream of water spilled into the bucket.

"Water looks good like thees," Carlos said.

"See? It sounds good too. It sounds like the word for this. Splash. Like slap."

"Splash," he said. "Good. Splashing, splashing." I could see that he got it.

We sat at the table and chatted when we returned to the cabin. Carlos seemed to grasp more and say more every day. "I was about as wild as you are when I was up here."

"Wild Jeri," he said with amusement.

I looked out the window. It was late summer but the larspur was still abundant. "I played day and night in that meadow and fished in the creek where those willows are," I told him. "This is the third summer I've known you, kid."

"Kid," he repeated with a snicker. "How many people here?"

"Here? When I was little? In the summer there were many people. My grandmother and grandfather lived here, and sometimes my parents came up with me and my brother. I would stay whenever I could."

"Stay here?" he asked.

"Yes, I'd stay here with my grandparents in the summer. My brother was always with me. It was like a little village. Do you know this word—village? Little town, very little town. There were cabins like this along the road down here, five cabins for my grandfather and his four brothers." I took him out on the porch and pointed west. "And there were more cabins up on the hill, about ten of them, maybe fifteen."

We turned to look out over the meadow, and I told him there had been a little store and a gas pump at the end of it and to the north of them, the sawmill. "Drove my grandfather's pickup truck when I was ten," I told him, and wished I hadn't.

We walked out into the meadow and picked a few lupines and Indian paintbrush and mule's ears—the yellow flower that was so pungent. The columbines my grandmother loved were finished blooming except in very sheltered places. When we had a handful, we took our flowers inside and stood them in a jar and poured in some of our drinking water.

"You like thees," Carlos said.

"I like it all up here."

"How soon here?" he asked.

"How soon? How young was I?"

"Young. First time?"

"I remember being here when I was four. My mother was pregnant." I put my hands over my stomach. "She fell in the woodshed. She stumbled over the wood and had a jolt and my brother jumped out early—my brother Robert Sinclair."

"Baby jumped out!" he laughed.

"He did. He jumped out completely early. Everyone said he looked like a baby rabbit. My mother barely got to the doctor in time. And when he got out of his incubator—a warm place for tiny babies—we came up here. We were all here from the beginning."

"Beautiful story," he told me.

I loved that. *Beautiful story.* Those days had been in many ways my most beautiful time.

"You crazy for thees cabin, Jeri," Carlos said. There was real fondness in his voice.

"Fully crazy," I said. "More than for anything there is."

"Why you not living here?" Deeply to the point—that was Carlos.

"Because my job isn't here," I said, thinking how lame an answer it was and what the real answer would be.

"Nothing work," he said. "You told me—live like animals."

"I misled you. I'm afraid the animals up here work pretty hard. Hey, I'm very hungry."

"Me too," he said and we made hamburgers and stacked them with tomatoes and lettuce and carried them on paper plates to my grandmother's kitchen window and ate our dinner.

"Delicious," Carlos said.

"Everything you cook on that wood fire will be delicious."

"I very like thees."

"It's peaceful here. Still and soft." We strolled out to the millpond.

"Grass and mint and brook," I said to him as we crossed over the little bridge. I walked logs for him, showing off—spinning them and hopping from one to the other like a lumberjack. "How you learn turn and jump?" he asked. "Will try."

"Just come out here on this big one, don't get off it. We don't have extra clothes for you if you fall in."

When we were back in the cabin, we made a fire in the fireplace. Carlos was astounded at life lived in the forest—hauling water, chopping wood, building fires. "Movie," he said.

"Yes," I told him, "you're in a western. The last of the westerns." He fell asleep in my grandfather's winged-back chair. He was still small enough that I could carry him into his bed.

I had bacon frying when he came out of his room the next morning. "Nothing afraid at night," he said, climbing up on the stool beside the stove.

"Are you sometimes afraid at night?" I asked.

"Yes. Meybe someone come," and he stepped away from the stool and did his cat-robber walk. "Meybe nothing hear."

I looked at him. *Protect him*, I said to myself. "Want to go to West Yellowstone?" I asked him as we ate. "It's not very far."

On the way, we stopped at the Continental Divide to contemplate the routes of water. We poked around West Yellowstone for a while but none of the shops were open. "We might as well go into the Park. You'd better see Old Faithful."

"Old Faithful," he repeated, and we went back to the car and drove through the big gate, and he read the signs on that scenic drive: Norris Junction, Firehole Campground Road, the Painted Pots or something like that, and then the splendid Old Faithful Inn. He looked up just in time to see the geyser keep her promise. He was transfigured.

"Not a lie?" he said to me.

"Not a lie," I answered.

When we were back in Utah, Carlos said, "Will come Friday or Saturday."

"Come Friday," I told him. "I will be with Karl Saturday." He began to do an imitation of Karl, and I interrupted it. "Come Friday," I said.

He was beside himself with excitement when he got off his bike at my place early Friday evening. You would have thought it was the first time he'd been to visit me. He ripped through the house, touching and naming everything until he could do something with his pleasure besides prance. I'd almost forgotten his old rambunctiousness. When he calmed down, we made tacos and chattered. He stood beside me at the kitchen counter, grating cheese and slicing tomatoes, sliding into his well-refined parody of a French chef sharpening his knife, eyebrows lifted, lips pursed.

Carlos's response to my unexpected decision to move to Montreal stayed the same. Every few days he made an improvement on the drawing he had begun when I first told him of my plans. In it he transported me along with all his classmates in what can only be called a hilarity-ridden bus. When I saw it, I realized I hadn't really known how to think of leaving him.

The last time we made tacos, it was a complete production. When everything was prepared, we shifted into a ceremonious tone, laying out colorful blue-and-orange Mediterranean placemats and yellow Fiesta dishes. We went out into the garden and clipped a few roses, brought them inside and plopped them in an old milk bottle and put them on the table. Then we sat down together and ate many tacos. After we got tired of being elegant (the irony of elegance at a taco party was not lost on us), Carlos initiated our best extension of the old game—how high *can* you toss a tortilla? You could see an idea overtake him, and just before the stroke of nine, he positioned himself, waited, and as the chimes struck, landed a taco flat on the cuckoo bird who hopped out on schedule. I was still laughing when he produced the now-finished drawing of the bus on its way to Montreal.

"We will be happy," he said as he handed the drawing to me. "Long time with." I stopped to consider—I would be twenty-eight in October and he would be fourteen in November. Some crucial years were going by for both of us.

Carlos's mind was on the present. He saw no reason why the trip to Montreal shouldn't be the grandest junket of all.

"You same crazy."

I WAS TIRED when I went to tell Carlos goodbye. I'd spent the evening before with Karl, and then I'd sat at my desk into the late hours, thinking of what I was doing. When I got to the now-faded turquoise house on Patterson Avenue, Lilly told me Carlos wasn't home. "He was sure sorry but he went with his Aunt Rose," she told me.

As I drove away from his house, I felt old—too old to be leaving my full world for some half-hearted retreat to a half-French city. Time to settle down and I was still scampering around like I'd done when I was twenty. What glittered before me when I'd said yes to teaching in Montreal felt flat and circumscribing on that day of leave-taking.

And Carlos hadn't been able to see me off. Did that mean he *was* busy, or too grieved? Karl would get along better. I was certain he would find someone more—*simpatica.* But that was to be another of life's certainties that would get adjusted.

I drove to Montreal with my dog, Mouse. Eugene had to be farmed out. It's actually a big deal to tell a parrot goodbye, not least because he is talking to you. It did end up being a six-day drive, with stops every hundred miles or so to check the trailer in which I was hauling a few possessions. The peace of being alone led me to take my time. It was a great, quiet rest, and I realized I hadn't had much of that. I drove through Idaho, where I spent a night at the cabin. The August evening had a hint of winter in it, and I saw that the ground cover was already turning gold and a few Oregon grape leaves had made their shift to scarlet. I tried not to notice too much or I'd never have left.

I ate breakfast in West Yellowstone the next morning and thought about Carlos and how he would fare. When I returned to my car, I sat in it and saw myself turning around and going back to Utah. But I put the car into gear and drove up over the Rockies and into the searing heat of Miles City. When I got to Fargo, I felt a serious pang at leaving the West. I wondered where the line was—had I already crossed it?

I must have slept through Minnesota and Wisconsin. I'd had to dull myself down. Then suddenly I was at the bridge in Sault Ste. Marie and dropping into Ontario, thinking once again of fur traders and explorers and fathers, this time Jesuit priests. Then I was back to wondering how I could manage to stay in close touch with Carlos. When I turned onto the King's Highway, I paid full attention to driving. Even so, my entrance into the province of Quebec and the vast city of Montreal was beyond uneven. I somehow found my way to Earnscliffe Drive and the apartment I'd rented. I lay in bed that night and listened to busses brake and start on the metropolitan street below, and I remembered how quiet my Utah house was in the evening and felt the knife of homesickness.

I couldn't have imagined I'd be with Karl only once more. Nor could I have guessed how much of Carlos I would see. But at first all the connections to my little deaf lad seemed to have been broken. Since there was no calling him, it was as though that voice of his, always on the brink of discovery, had left the world.

I gazed out over Montreal from the fifteenth floor of my high-rise, went to the docks to look for captain's chairs, found the Customs House and claimed a few things. I walked my dog in Mount Royal Park two or three times a day. I fell in love immediately with my new students—younger than any I'd taught, and endearing.

Then a letter came from Carlos, obviously written at school and corrected until not much of his color remained. In fact, I could find almost nothing left of him in it, and so it was bittersweet to read.

Finally one came from his home, where he had had less help, and a great deal more was revealed. "I'm doing fine in school," he wrote. "I wait for my Mother in principals office so I will not get in trouble." It was signed "I love you, Carlos Louis Salazar."

At the bottom of the page was a note from Lilly. She said Carlos was so sorry he didn't get to see me before I left. It was the first note I had had from her, and I was interested in her graceful handwriting and her signature—Mrs. Salazar.

The next news about Carlos came from the handsome, good-hearted principal of the School for the Deaf. Over the years I had known Carlos, we had come to be warm friends. His letter was full of the irresistible mix of ingenuousness and unusual caring I'd come to like. In it he thanked me for writing to Carlos, assuring me that my letters meant a great deal to him. I read and re-read what he went on to say:

> He is having more complex problems this year since, of course, he does not have you to lean on. I was down to his home several weeks ago and I noticed your picture on the dresser. The family adores you.
>
> It is with deep regret that I pass this additional information on to you. We feel Carlos is continually regressing in his outside experiences. The latest report that I gained is that he is now involved in stealing from grocery stores downtown. Of course, I cannot confirm this because at this time he has not been caught in this misdemeanor. I don't know how you would go about making such a comment to him, but he is only going to get in trouble if he continues to do this. It may be that you will want to continue writing in the positive nature of what you and he did last year.
>
> I think the greatest asset that he has at this time is just hearing from you. He just seems to radiate when he receives an envelope from Montreal.

I was alarmed. I was touched. And I was helpless except for the letters I did write. It was all I could do not to get in the car and drive back to Utah. I wondered if I'd underestimated my role. I don't think I'd really seen myself as that significant an influence on Carlos; I'd seen him as a friend and a delight. I suppose I had in large measure seen him from my point of view—what he meant to me. I would not have presumed to think of myself as a crucial person to him.

Sometimes we ask for what we really want. We set aside pattern and custom and articulate some dream below the surface of daily life. I did that. I wrote to Lilly and said send Carlos if he'd like to come for a few weeks or a month. I knew that he could fly out after Christmas vacation with someone we both happened to know. One of the teachers from the Utah School for the Deaf would be returning to Montreal to be principal of the Montreal Oral School for the Deaf. It would be easy and Carlos wouldn't have to fly alone. He could attend classes at the school while he visited, and be among friends in the bargain. The school I taught in was nearby.

Lilly wrote back at once:

> I received your letter, sure was a pleasure to hear from you we are o.k. hope you are alright.
>
> Thought I would answer right away. Carlos says yes, So you can go ahead and send the airplane ticket. Will close for now.
>
> Till I hear from you Again
>
> Answer soon.

Carlos says yes rang through the entire lovely old city of Montreal. How vivid it suddenly became as I re-assessed it all, imagining it as he would see it. First we would drive along the magnificent boulevards that curved through the city. Then we would chase squirrels in Mount Royal Park. He would see the men in their lamb's wool hats, ear flaps lowered and the heavy collars of their coats turned up as they hurried through the great flakes of snow that hadn't stopped falling since the middle of December. We would go to the St. Lawrence and poke around the customs houses and the docks and watch the huge barges come down the seaway. We'd have a cup of hot chocolate in the St.

Regis and Carlos would be amazed that the biggest hotel in Ogden would fit in its splendid lobby. He had never seen a building higher than twenty stories, and he would be almost that high in my apartment in Earnscliffe Towers, with twenty stories still above him.

I don't think I'd imagined that Carlos would say yes. Might as well write to a colt and say *come out*, I'd thought as I was doing it. I knew he wasn't much for leaving Patterson Avenue. But he *was* coming, and I let my imagination run free. When I walked my dog in the park that evening, I could see Carlos laughing at the squirrels scampering along the sidewalks of St. Mary's as they maneuvered between the cars and busses and endless people. What would he make of French on half a coin, half a can, half a sign, and well over half the lips of the Québécois? The quaintness, the grandness, the eloquence of Montreal—every difference was registered by me anew as I waited for the raven prince from Utah to come.

He stepped off the red, white, and blue Boeing 707 looking frail and overwhelmed and greeted me with a shy, perfunctory hug. I had never seen him so solemn. In fact, except for that one terrible moment when he had taken Marian's money, I had never seen him the least bit solemn. I noticed with a shock that he had scarcely grown, scarcely changed, since I had first seen him four years ago.

Hardly saying a word, we went to get his luggage and then walked side by side to my red Mustang. I couldn't stand our politeness and, worse, nervousness, so I suddenly fell into my old ruse, dropping to the ground—heels, dress, suede coat be damned—in my elaborate faux faint. The ploy was straight out of a forties movie. Lana Turner. As many times as I had done it, it had always fairly killed him off. I had overused it a good deal once I had perfected it, so I'd had to get more and more elaborate to make it work. The thing was to do it with fabulous timing and at an absolutely horrendous moment—so unexpected and inappropriate that the first thought would always be, "This time she has really collapsed."

I had nearly gotten tangled in Carlos's suitcase on my way down, but I'd cleared it at the last minute. Not another second later, Carlos was on his knees, face white but slightly—yes, I was sure it was slightly expectant.

When the expectation subsided and alarm was at its height, I opened my eyes with all the gotcha nature I had and said that heavily deployed line of ours. The "'*allo BA-by!*' did its work, and I watched him fill with admiration.

He buried his face against my fur collar and murmured, "Miss you, miss you, miss you," and I laughed and struggled up and congratulated myself on managing, once more, to have captivated him.

He stood back from me, doing a full survey, and said, "You same crazy!" and we raced to the car, forgetting the suitcase. When we returned for it, we couldn't find it, so after a while we went back to the airport and had hot dogs and then ice cream cones. When we came out again, we went right to the suitcase, loaded it into the Mustang, and drove through the falling twilight toward Earnscliffe Towers. A name like that goes far back in time, I thought. It's right out of *Wuthering Heights.* We laughed all the way home.

In the months that Carlos stayed in Montreal, he changed his life. He introduced himself at school as Louis Salazar and filled out all his entry forms and answered all questions about himself with a few new facts: he was twelve now, not his actual thirteen. Thereafter he insisted he had been twelve when he was in Montreal, although many years later he was to put his age then as fourteen in a chronology he made of his life. I never found reason to contradict him, particularly since he was placed in a class with ten- and twelve-year-olds, whose size and abilities he approximated.

Before he started school, we went downtown to buy him a blue blazer and gray slacks, the uniform he would wear. Tongue cannot tell how I loved that day. That was the day I felt fully like a mother, not a buddy. I was shopping with him and he was delighted. He put on those gray pants and a white shirt and the navy blazer, and our salesman excused himself and returned with a tie and said, "These are the colors of your school, Carlos."

As we wandered through the handsome stores, he looked about with the pert fascination I'd loved in him when we'd taken our first trip to the mountains. If something caught his attention, his head would move to one side, birdlike, his eyebrows would lift, and he would study it as though there were nothing else in the world. We found a schoolbag embossed with the provincial crest of Quebec. It had five pockets, one of them secret, which Carlos found and examined for a considerable time. No one in Utah ever carried schoolbags, but he went off his first day looking as though he had never not carried one. He could always pick up, down to the slightest detail, the prevailing look of any given group and, if he chose, not only imitate it but improve upon it.

Monday morning Carlos announced himself at the Montreal Oral School for the Deaf with something beyond aplomb. He could have been the prime minister's son. I took him to his classroom, so I had occasion to stand in the back and watch what happened. It is one of those images I can replay perfectly. He has on his freshly pressed gray pants, the crisp, long-sleeved white shirt, the blue-and-yellow school tie, and the beautifully styled blue blazer. No one else in the room seems to be wearing what Carlos is wearing, but they are, yet they look common and rumpled.

He walks to the front of the class and stands before the teacher, who is clearly struck by him. His black hair is neatly parted on one side, a little tuft of wave combed to the other side. His jacket is open, and his white shirt frames his face, making his brown eyes and black lashes even more dramatic. His skin has that olive creamy tone I've always thought everyone wants.

"'Allo, I'm Louis Salazar," he says , the voice trailing out—*Lou-is,* and here his voice goes high—*Sal-a-zar.* He puts out his hand to be shaken. I don't know where any of this comes from. I can see the teacher dissolve. His speech, I later learn, is the best in the class. Every student watches him, entranced—round little Rowena; tall, confident Dave; pretty Louise; strong, bullying Bud; soggy, drenchy Ralph; and all the others I don't come to know as well.

"Welcome," says his teacher, Lydia. As soon as we get home, we say it like the British Canadians do—*Lyd-j-ia.*

"Welcome!" she says, and she means it, and I sneak out of the classroom feeling the pleasure of being endowed with a handsome, charming son.

Driving home, I am smiling. I can't believe that is the boy who wore his shirt unbuttoned to the navel, who darted into grocery stores and shot a hand into the till, who tore out into the alley and down to the river bottom.

I was just smart enough to fear for how different his worlds were. I had no idea that in a few years I would spend many hours in a hospital room talking to him about this time of fullness and wholeness so that he would not lose track of himself as he was before medications made him almost unrecognizable.

Even after watching that first fifteen minutes in his classroom, I still wasn't prepared for Carlos's newest role. His manners remained elaborate, his dress meticulous. He fairly wore me out ironing white shirts and gray pants. He was for the first time in his life—and apparently without effort—the best student in his room. And he was unquestionably everyone's favorite. Girls fell irretrievably in love with him. Boys admired and eventually envied him. Those he favored he brought home for cupcakes and milk and a view from our balcony of the white hills of Mount Royal Park.

The rough-and-tumble Utah days of furiously and endlessly playing games of hide-and-go-seek that left every object within hailing distance chipped, broken, or up-ended were over. Except when we were alone and got to acting crazy, Carlos was an engaging, budding young boy journeying toward manhood.

"Up with everything."

LOUIS, AS HE NOW IDENTIFIED HIMSELF, had spent too many days and nights at my house in Utah for there to be any real adjustment in his arrival in Montreal. We fitted back together as though there had been no break in time or place. After having had just myself to take care of, I relished the chores brought by a boy hungry for dinner or waiting for his shirt to be pressed. I'd wanted seven of them from the day I'd met Jo in *Little Women*.

Among the best times we had in Montreal were walks in the park when we both got home from our separate schools, which were, luckily, only about twenty blocks apart. My dog would be waiting with desperation when we came in the door. We'd throw on our warmest clothes, sometimes grab our ice skates, and march off with the dog straining at his leash and heavily favoring me. He would never walk beside Carlos, and he never let him forget what the hierarchy was.

Carlos was enthralled with the sweep and surge of city life. So was I. We took it in like urban pilgrims—discovering the department store in an all but residential area and right next to it the deli, and the hardware store on the corner, none of it ten minutes from our high-rise. Along the way, Carlos would fetch a jaunty drawing from his pocket that illustrated his day's finest moment. Often there was some note of endearment, stamped with his high style.

One particularly cold day, Carlos and I were huddled on a park bench when a puffy woman in a white Persian lamb coat came along with a fancy bit of a dog. She let him loose and joined us on the bench, acknowledging me, and then turned to talk to Carlos in the grand manner some adults use with children. Such occasions were agony for him. I could almost see questions formulating in his mind, and I remembered the sign on his back—*Deaf Carlos.* Would he be able to speechread a stranger? Would she understand him if he did answer? Or, worst of all, would she speak French? All his dash would evaporate in seconds in such a situation, leaving him shuffling, head ducked, and yes, mute.

He turned awkwardly away from her. "Rude!" she said to both of us. I stood up and joined Carlos, calling Mouse as I did so.

"Mouse?" she voiced, sounding like Eleanor Roosevelt, a shocked Eleanor Roosevelt. "What an odd name for a dog."

Unbearably prim, she called "Here Bunny, here Bunny," in that scratching, sing-song voice. I collapsed in laughter. Carlos was better at disguising his snickers—which always came when mine did—as we ran along after Mouse, me trying to tell him what she'd said but unable to get it out until we were home. He got to be as good with the line "Here Bunny, here Bunny" as she'd been, although his ironic edge was somewhere she'd never get.

A curious mix of Carlos's two identities at the time was in one of the inimitable letters he let flutter into every room of the house. In it he explained in parentheses that "I" refers to Carlos, but the signature remained Louis, as it did on almost everything he wrote or drew in Montreal.

Dear Jeri,

Hi, Jeri.

You like Mouse. I (Carlos) like Mouse.

I love Jeri. Very very very much.

I love two.

LOVE,

Louis

Was he reinventing himself—as mysterious and unavoidable as any rebirth, the chrysalis inevitable as he stepped into the boy he wanted to be? Or was he involved in theater, exercising his audacity? Was there some element of being the boy he thought I wanted?

As the days passed, Carlos and I avoided counting them or talking about how long his "visit" should last. We just kept on plundering the city for adventures. If we didn't go skating on one of the nearby rinks or walk Mouse in the park after school, we'd take the new metro downtown and shop. We went to antique car shows, airplane shows, churches older than our own nation, and we ate every kind of food we could find—couscous and *coq au vin* and tabbouleh and tagine and good old chop suey.

All the time we talked and talked, and Carlos mused at the world and all the words he was learning to describe it. Language—watching him learn it—was like running a hand through jewels. I began to wonder if language shapes one's personality or adorns it. I thought on and off in those years that it was the deepest means by which we create ourselves. Now I'm back to not being so sure. I think Carlos could have been Carlos with the rise and fall of a shoulder or eyebrow, the tilt of his head. He would have continued to add to that repertoire. Would the thought process have been circumscribed? We might end up thinking that words do that as well.

It was in these months that Carlos began not only to talk easily and freely but to become understandable to almost everyone. When we weren't exploring Montreal's parks and docks and museums, we sat in the living room looking out toward St. Joseph's Cathedral in Mount Royal Park and chatted by the hour. And always there were his wonderful drawings, sometimes with stories he'd composed at school.

Carlos, as I knew he would be, was hilarious to live with. His amusing touch could be encountered in the least expected places. Once I went looking for him in his room early one evening and just as I was about to turn on the light, I felt a piece of paper covering the switch. I ran my hand over it and came to a little hole cut out around the switch itself. I realized this was a tape-up job, a specialty of his, and with what

I was very tired.

Move back
The car almost hit me
Miss Parker saw me.
She yelled, "Move back!"
I didn't see the car.

light came from the hall, I peeped at the words he'd written until I could make out the message:

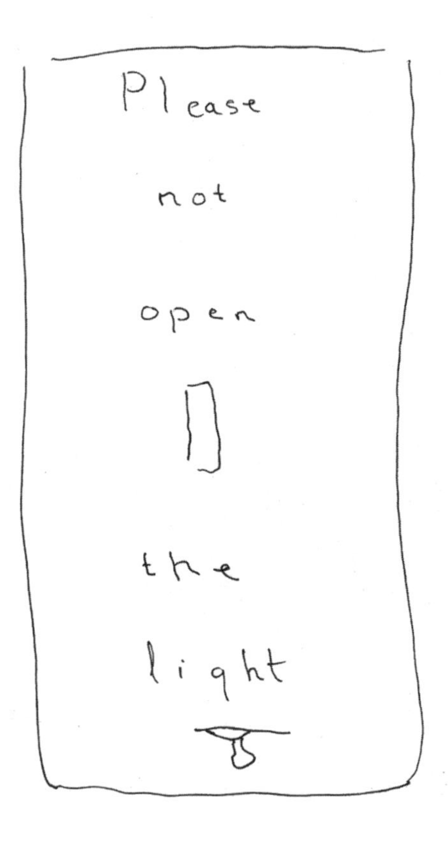

I've turned that phrase over in my mind for a lot of years. His invented language always had a whimsy to it. But I deliberated on this one. I'm sure I took the message beyond what he intended. It was a practical message here, but still, behind "not open the light" was its reverse. And I could hear the King James language I loved: "If therefore the light that is in thee be darkness, how great is that darkness."

Carlos compelled me. I went to bed in the dark, thinking that opening the light was his greatest gift.

A saying current at the time fascinated Carlos. I think it was his first full discovery of the fun of idioms, although I had had him saying for years, "Get hoppin'," "Perk up," "Hang it all," and his favorite, "You're driving me crackers," which he had, characteristically, personalized to "You're driving me nervous."

The expression of the day in Montreal was "Up with everything!" Popular as it was, and essentially stupid as it was, it was used in a wretchedly narrow sense, as all clichés come to be. Carlos, however, felt no such constraints. For him, "Up with everything!" applied to a thousand situations, most of them way outside regular adaptations. If I was downhearted or poky for some reason, he would toss an arm about me and chirp, "Up with everything!"—his manner so earnest, yet so amused, I would burst out laughing.

Carlos was particularly interested in one area of language at that time. He was almost fifteen by then, although he was still very small. But life was surging along in him, and he asked *every* question about his body and its functions. One day he climbed up in my burgundy rocking chair to sit beside me—there was plenty of room for both of us—and he plunked a dictionary in my lap. "What name?" he said, starting with his hair and working from there down his body, every fingernail taken into consideration. If he didn't know the word or the spelling of it, he helped me find it in the dictionary and drew a red line under it.

When we got to the parts of his body that were of surpassing interest to him at the time, that had no doubt inspired this exercise, my words invariably differed from those he had learned from his friends at home. He would write what he had learned and then write the word I told him beside it, causing me not a few uncomfortable moments. His terms weren't just standard-issue neighborhood words. What I was looking at was hard street talk. "Don't be a ridiculous old nun," I told myself, refusing to let my eyes leave the page until I was sure I could be quite casual. Even now I'd have trouble writing the street word for vagina.

He said, "What's it for?" confused about why there were two sets of words. How to explain the silliness of "proper" English and—what, vulgate? But there it was. It probably was the clearest line drawn in the sand between our different worlds. We spoke, on this point, different languages. I studied the two columns of words. Was there different intent as well as vocabulary? I tried to tell him it was like a doctor and a patient. The doctor would use a word he had learned at school. The patient would use a word he had learned at home. They meant the same thing. I illustrated it with an example he knew—that of vomiting versus throwing up—trying every way I could not to make one set of terms seem preferable to another. It was a weak example, I had that figured out at once, and a pitched example. The doctor held higher ground. And as squeamish as I was, I couldn't stand to strengthen my point by bringing up the third, even more colloquial, term. I didn't want to make much of the point anyway. Above all, I did not want him to return to the world he would go back to a snob, or worse, a critic of it. For one thing, my own world was beginning to look pretty anemic to me.

Not long after that, Carlos came out of the bathroom, swept a hand across the front of his pants, and said quizzically, "What's it for—up with everything?" identifying that unmistakable masculine phenomenon with a gesture all his own. I laughed heartily at this newest application of his by-now indispensable phrase, and then attempted to sail into an explanation with as much ease and humor as he brought to the discussion. I wish I could remember what I said. I had not given a thought to how I'd explain the advent of erections. Was it more of a surprise to Carlos than to others? Or was he purposely finding an occasion to have this fact between us?

I did my best with his candid curiosity and questions in the months that followed, learning a good deal about my own sense of propriety and its fetters and sometimes tyranny over the individual. Nothing could have given more insight into the urgencies and comedies of life than providing Carlos with language for his excursion through adolescence. At the end of that circuitous passage, I could see that standing in its way would have been to tangle with a force of nature.

The only day Carlos fell back into his old "trouble at school" in Montreal nearly broke his heart. He had provoked his classmates to rowdiness, and our friend Stan, who was the principal, had had to discipline him. It was the first trouble Carlos had encountered since he'd left the stucco house on Patterson Avenue. When he didn't come home and it began to get late, I called Stan. He told me he had given Carlos a little paddling—people still did that in those days—and that Carlos had accepted it with anguish rather than what we had all come to call his Utah starch.

I waited another half hour. The only good thought I had was that at least we weren't in the same school and I had a little distance from his life there. As the minutes went by, I felt for the first time the frantic helplessness of trying to find him out there in a city of two million, a city that I could easily be lost in myself, a city turning to shadows and phantoms now.

The phone rang and I flew to it. I had taught Carlos how to use it in the limited way that he could. In countless practices, he would go downstairs to the lobby phone and dial my number, wait a moment, and then say, "'allo. I am downstairs. I am coming up," and hang up. I had wanted him to know that, while he could hear no response, he could give a message.

By the time I got the phone off the receiver, he was already talking. His voice came between sobs. "Trouble again. Trouble in school." Silence and sobs and then, "I was down with everything," and the line went dead.

Something deep in me stumbled. I tried to think what he would do, where he would go to seek comfort and find refuge from himself. What if he ran, this time into some unknown section of a dark city, not his familiar fields and foothills?

The phone rang again, and this time I had it off the hook before Carlos began talking. "I was very sad. I was downstairs alone. I was to Parker's car."

By the time the line went dead again, I was in the hallway, tearing for the elevator. I pushed the button, but instead of waiting, I decided to take the seventeen flights of stairs to the underground garage where my car was.

I couldn't see anyone in the Mustang as I approached it, but I went over to it anyway. There, barely visible on the floor of the front passenger seat, was a white shirt, dark head bent over the seat, and I saw that my little Carlos had come to confront his heartbreak with himself rather than flee into his now-distant hills.

I opened the door and sat down on the edge of the seat. Carlos lifted a tear-soaked face into my lap and wept violently. What had he hoped for himself that he wouldn't arrive at? Or had sabotaged? When we went upstairs, his body was still trembling from the sobs that continued to run through him like earthquakes.

“Wow very POW!”

CARLOS ALWAYS KEPT the rare ability to fire in the mind an image that would endure for decades, undiminished. And he was as memorable when he was the serpent in the garden as when he was the bloom.

From time to time he would get angry enough to trot out what was to become his favorite threat, “I’m go back to Utah!” He never said, “I want my mother,” or “I’m homesick,” although looking back I’m sure at times he did want his mother and was homesick. But his main references to Utah were made as though it were a tool, and he knew how to wield it to advantage. Pale with fury when he would threaten, he would set his jaw and glower at me.

At first I’d say, “You can go back, Carlos. You can fly back when you’re ready.” That wasn’t what he wanted. He finally had me saying, “How are you getting to Utah?” playing right into his hands.

“Walk!” he would exclaim. Usually at such moments he was still so lovable, my own vexation would fall away, and I’d have to stop myself from hugging him beyond his petulance.

But occasionally it seemed like more than a good idea to both of us, and I would snap, “Fine! I’ll help you pack! Where’s your suitcase? And hey, you’d better carry a lot of food; it will take you until summer to get there! If you don’t get lost!” Hardly my proudest moment.

“I don’t care!” would come lashing back, uttered with true not caring.

Once when I was particularly exhausted from the run of sleeplessness that would periodically hit Carlos, and with him the household, I left the apartment. I had a bad moment of wondering whether he would be afraid to be alone in it, but I marched out anyway. An hour later, as I was returning—I had hardly gotten out of sight of the exit from our building—I saw Carlos below me on the stairway between the bank and the Viennese restaurant we often went to. He had Mouse on a leash and was leaning over him, murmuring, "Smell, Mouse, smell Jeri. Find Jeri. Find."

Over and over he pointed to his nose and sniffed frantically, then tried, by means of maneuvering the leash, to get Mouse to lower his head and pick up the scent. Mouse, who had never traced more than a T-bone before, grew more and more bewildered as Carlos urged him with increasing desperation.

Carlos was entirely beside himself when he looked up to see me watching him. "Too many people!" he said in exasperation. "Almost lost!" He was so relieved to see that *I* hadn't gone back to Utah, or that neither of us were forever lost, he didn't mind having been found in what was pretty close to urgent repentance.

One evening he popped up from before the television and his beloved *Mission: Impossible* series to disappear for nearly half an hour. I was about to go in search of him when suddenly out of his room whirled a tiny little Arab draped in black, an elaborate headdress wrapped about his dark, delicate face. He sat in the center of the living room floor, deep in a mystical state by the time he had crossed his legs. He began at once to pipe away on an imaginary instrument, his body weaving like a reed as he played sweetly to a snake in the make-believe basket between his knees.

When I was able to talk between gasps of laughter, I asked him what he was doing. I knew perfectly well, but I wanted to hear how he would describe the endeavor. "Charming up the worm," he answered, the chirp of his voice moving to its steadily lower range, and I was off again.

On another occasion I walked into the living room to see a nattering old lady, glasses down over her nose. Her hair would have been back in a bun, you could tell that. She sat in a big rocking chair, entirely unaware of me, and knit away busily, nearly blindly. Not until I sobbed with laughter yet again did the boy break out of his old-lady cocoon.

The memorable images were everywhere on paper. "My Jeri scolded me," he wrote as the theme of one bit of homework—I've forgotten what the provocation was. But what he put his mind to when he came home that day said far more. He drew a picture of a mother eagle exercising fearful unrighteous dominion over her baby, still a chick and one not entirely out of his shell. Written above the deeply wronged chick's head was "Wow very POW!"

"Nothing home."

I WASN'T SURPRISED that the sublime spirit Carlos and I brought to each other's lives affected more than just the positive realm. Of course there was the inevitable compound—the dark hours as well as the dear ones. I had that figured out long before I knew him.

Still, it was always hard for me to lose the easy grace with Carlos, even for short periods. If his happiness made me glow, his wrath dimmed the sun. I did what most mothers—and I suppose surrogate mothers—of that era did. I determined that it was nonsense to let a child dictate my moods and resolved not to be awash in his currents. Interestingly, a third person put that resolve to the test, albeit inadvertently.

"I'm going to the hockey game with my friend Serge Saturday night," I told Carlos one evening when he had been in Montreal about three weeks. "You met Serge in the restaurant. Do you remember him?"

Carlos shrugged his shoulders, his way of letting me know he didn't understand, or didn't care. Or didn't want me to think he cared. Unlike most of his gestures, this one was slow. In fact he seemed almost to hang suspended in it until I went on to explain.

"Remember the tall man with the German shepherd?"

"Een the car?" Carlos asked. Serge's dog Brutus virtually lived in Serge's car when he was at work. After dinner that night, we had accompanied Serge to the underground parking area where his dog was waiting. As soon as we left the elevator, Serge began speaking to his dog, even though we had to turn a corner before we could see the dog through the window of the car. "Brutus!" he repeated over and over, chuckling between utterances. He said it in mock sternness. "Brutus!" The excitement of a boy was in that big voice. By the time we could see the car, Brutus was in a nervous ecstasy.

"Brutus!" Serge exclaimed one last time. "It's time for your dinner, girl." By then he had the car opened, and the dog was at his feet, whimpering with joy.

"Brutus is a girl?" I laughed. The bond between him and his dog aroused pleasure and respect in me. Carlos sensed it, and I could feel him move outside the connection.

Still Carlos was fascinated as Serge opened his trunk, took out two cans of dog food from a half-empty case of it, produced a can opener from who knows where, and closed the trunk. He placed one can of dog food on the rear fender of his deep green racing car—it was a very souped-up outfit—and then opened both ends of the other can. All the while he murmured about the delights of dinnertime to his dog, whose breathing and motions were becoming almost frenzied. "Brutus! Beefsteak, Brutus. Dinner for you, Brutus!"

He then removed the rim of one end of the can and fitted it neatly over the other end. He placed his two large thumbs over the combined lids and pushed until a tube of dog food emerged from the open end. It was done as deftly as though it were nothing more than a tube of toothpaste. Through the process, Carlos remained silent but fascinated in spite of himself.

Brutus had begun to whine and shift her weight. "Brutus!" Serge bellowed. The dog sat instantly and Serge held the tube of dog food toward her. Brutus ate it neatly, almost in one gulp. The process was repeated with the second can. Not a morsel of the food touched Serge's hand, or the garage floor.

Carlos finally let himself admire the whole ritual, and I had hoped he would like Serge, who was a hearty, warm man.

Now, as our words hung in the air, I could see Carlos remember Serge. The moment he made the connection, he picked up the homework he'd been dabbling at and went with great dignity and finality to his bedroom.

"I won't be home after school," he said the next morning at breakfast. It was all he said.

"You mean you'll be late?" I asked him.

"Nothing home," he said.

"Are you going to sleep on your desk?" I tried.

"No," he responded. "Other."

"Where *are* you going to sleep?" I asked, beginning to get annoyed.

"With friend," was all he would offer. I noticed his language deteriorating as it always did when he was angry or worried. He was already late for school, so I sent him on his way. I wanted the day to figure this one out.

As soon as he was gone, I filled with dread. Suppose he didn't come home? If he were my boy, really, I might let him huff off and find out how twenty-four hours of that felt. But he wasn't my boy—he was Lilly's. Suppose he got on a bus and didn't—

"Ridiculous," I interrupted myself. "Carlos isn't going to do anything to hurt Carlos." But despite the assurances I gave myself, I only barely got through the lunch hour without going to his school. When his last bell sounded at 3:30, I was standing outside his classroom door.

He came tumbling out, his old impudence first. Gone for the moment was the gentleman he'd become, and in its place was a strange little infidel.

I got a withering look for openers. Clearly I had broken some rule I hadn't had time to find out about. That his behavior toward me was shocking I could see in the faces of his friends, who had only known him to be courtly to me.

I waited for him to say something. He bumped past me without a word or a second look and was on his way down the stairs when Lydia, his teacher, came to the door.

"Did Carlos have a little electricity on his Cherrios this morning?" she said. "I thought he would fly into a million sparks before noon."

"Just about," I said.

"Well, whatever happened," she continued, "he was certainly different from the lord and leader he's always been. He fastened himself to

Jeffrey, who was thrilled, and just before school was out, he announced he was going home with him."

"The lad contains multitudes," I replied, wondering what Jeffrey's mother would do when she heard the news. By the time I got to the curb, she had identified me. "Oh, you take care of the little Salazar boy," she said. "Carlos just came right up to me and asked me if he could stay over tonight. I'm not prepared." I suppose my manner might have been as stiff as hers if her son had taken me by surprise. She looked as though Carlos had taken her hostage. I stood there wondering whether his being Spanish American was a factor—or maybe being American was enough.

I could have killed Carlos at that moment. He had taken public his anger at me, or, to name it more accurately, his jealousy toward Serge. What the hell did he want me to say to her, *Would two weeks be too long?*

"Swell," I mumbled and followed it quickly with, "I see," trying to bring a little equanimity to the situation. For the first time in my years with Carlos, I felt overwhelmed. I was aware that he stood twenty feet away, watching me. I suddenly missed him, missed our alliance as I realized he meant his presence to limit what I said.

Mrs. Redd, whom I envied for having had her boy's entire lifetime to learn how to manage this sort of thing, suddenly softened. She must have recognized that I was being punished, banished. "Tonight is a bad time," she turned and said to Carlos in slow and exaggerated speech. She turned back to me for an indication of whether he had understood. I nodded toward Carlos, and she continued, her voice as questioning as her words. "Would you come Friday night when I can make preparations?"

Ha! I thought, alas I did. I thought that ought to teach him. But before I looked at him, I'd already felt the pain of being so inadequate a mother. What he did next took my heart away. A tear shone in those indomitable eyes. "Never mind," he said, his head bowed so that he was almost inaudible. "Busy Friday," he said, even softer, as he turned and walked away. I began to reach for him but had the sense to let him go.

I was so unhappy with my having entered the contest, I too turned and left. He was a boy, I was a woman. He didn't know how to handle the world and its kaleidoscope of people and emotions. He wasn't being in a snit for the pleasure of it. One component was probably fear. Montreal was vast. He'd come from a town of sixty thousand, and that had been focused into one tightly woven neighborhood—one only in his lifetime.

I felt too low and inadequate even to think further. How could it possibly work for me to have Carlos here? His friends, his haunts—his whole world was two thousand miles away.

When I caught a glimpse of him on the drive home, he was standing with his back to the street, staring into a shop window. The line of his shoulder, the way his hair lay, announced that he was an orphan and desolate. I pulled over and suffered, but he was unapproachable as yet, and I had a great terror of his beginning to run, the immense city ready to swallow him.

I shuffled around the apartment that evening, torturing myself with how I had dislocated a boy. What he was going through out there along St. Mary's Way was unbearable to me. His capacity for shame and humiliation were highly developed. How had I forgotten that? I paced the apartment again.

What was I to do when he did come back? What would be the price to him if I stayed home this Saturday night? And next? And what would be the price to me? To us?

The difficulties of communicating with him dropped over me like a pall. If I could say to him, "We have our whole lives ahead of us. We both need separate lives. It will be too thin for you this way . . ." It would be tough enough to say, "I won't leave you alone. I'll take you to my friend's for the evening. Or to Jeffrey's."

Then I wondered if that wasn't all that could be said with words. My plans with Serge looked like a menace instead of a pleasure, and I longed for someone to talk to. What would my grandmother say to me? I wondered, remembering how seemingly casual she was in her mothering. *Don't get in the way.* I knew what she would say as soon as I thought of her. *Scratch your feelings together and let things work out.*

I went back to our apartment, made myself a cup of tea, and sat on the balcony looking out at the night lights. *Don't ever be too far, off,* I said to her.

a thousand voices

Carlos must have slept in the car until 2:00 a.m. At least he looked like he'd been asleep when he let himself into the apartment and into his room. The next morning he was gone when I woke up. He had left a note for me on his breakfast plate.

> Parker, I don't why. Will home tonight.
> I love you. I with you.
> Carlos Louis

Reading it, I thought how little I knew about how to use language.

"I will Utah now or jump."

WHAT WAS ALWAYS COMPELLING in Carlos was his intelligence, the lighthouse within him. It informed his sorrow as well as his celebration—kept his quiet from emptiness, his tenderness from softness, his urgency from frenzy. In almost all his attitudes, intelligence prevailed.

Many other things can be given or learned or even imitated. Intelligence is not among them. The ability Carlos had to combine and re-combine everything at hand into something new had its roots in intelligence. It was the force that drove him, even after his energy was gone. His phrases, his drawings, his yearnings all bore the stamp of his fierce—and perhaps in part because of his deafness—his free intelligence.

It's lucky he had it because he needed it. If he was able to re-create with language, to bring new combinations of words and feelings to the most usual of experiences; if his responses were as exceptional as, say, when he covered my eyes, not wanting me to hear; still he had a hundred moments in a day to leap the chasm of incomplete information. If behind him or beyond him, the signal of a voice would begin something or end it and he hadn't seen the words, he was excluded.

Half his life was inexplicable. He usually had to wonder why everyone suddenly put coats on, prepared to leave. He could easily miss the transitional phrase—I have to meet a train; I'm late to pick up my wife. Unseen or guessed-at links between cause and effect would always be what Carlos grappled with most rigorously. And when he failed to see connections, especially those that applied to the future as well as the present, he sometimes refused to go along with what he did not understand. If the confounding thing wasn't important to him, he simply withdrew. If it did matter, he could become stubborn and sometimes intractable.

Sleeping was, for example, a vast complexity between the two of us. From his point of view, what possible objection could there be to sleeping together? From mine, how could I possibly communicate all the objections? The practical ones were the easiest; the subtle and maybe foolish ones far beyond simply hard.

Of course he could not. That was all. At what age, once begun, would he wander back down the hall to his own room? Already at the end of his thirteenth year, he was no stranger to its adolescent buffetings. He could *not* sleep with me, his twenty-eight-year-old friend. But Carlos had almost always slept with his mother. In his very firm opinion, that was reason enough for him to sleep with me. How much actual sleep we both lost over the issue tongue cannot begin to tell.

So frequent were our bouts on the subject, it is practically impossible for me to separate out one incident and let it stand for the thousands of struggles that were struggled when night fell. Darkness must have been like a tunnel for Carlos—not only black but soundless as well. When the lights went out, so did his system of communication. He could not hear a scream or a call, let alone a comforting voice. Instead he was constantly startled.

Not surprisingly, he hated nights, keeping me up with him until his eyes would smart with the effort not to give in to sleep. He would run through the house, the dazed prankster trying to joke himself and me into one more hour of camaraderie. The real struggle would begin when, dazed myself, I finally dragged back to my room. Then Carlos would pop in to turn on the light and ask, "What clean shirt tomorrow?" We'd go through whether or not his white shirt was pressed, and he'd come sit on my bed and begin some elaborate tale. I'd be asleep in two lines, and he'd slither down beside me, quiet as a forbidden puppy. At other times I'd awaken at two or three in the morning to hear his breathing, deep and ragged beside me. At such moments my own confusion would swirl through me as I contemplated the cold little interloper, only wanting to be near someone who would hear what he didn't hear, who would get him through the night.

"I am close," I would assure him on the way back to his room. "I can hear you. Call me if you want me and I'll fly to you." I would end entreating and finally pleading with him to stay in his room, half mad from lack of sleep by the time he'd been in Montreal two weeks.

From time to time, and always unexpectedly, his endless efforts not to be left alone would turn to the white fury that could crush out everything else in him. The tightness would come to his mouth, the hardness to his eyes. "I will Utah in the morning," he'd hurl at me. "That's okay," I'd say, and later, after the first fifty times, I'd exclaim, "Okay! Your suitcase is in your closet."

One night I heard him go to his room and get his suitcase out. Concerned as I was, I fell asleep for what must have been an hour. When Carlos shoved at me roughly to waken me, he had his suitcase in his hand. He opened it to show me it contained only things I had given him—his cherished blazer and pants, a pair of brown-and-black leather ice skates, his white shirts and his tie, two pairs of pajamas, his schoolbag, his Boy Scout knife, his wallet. Nothing that had been a gift, a happy bond between us, was missing.

Five seconds after I'd looked into his suitcase with sleepy distress, he marched out onto the balcony with it, opened it, and scattered its contents, money included, down through the night. It all landed fifteen stories below on the roof of the entryway to our apartment building. Carlos looked at me, shivering and shocked in the winter night, and said with deadly good speech and pure intent, "I will Utah now or jump." If I had seen what I see now, I would have recognized a boy who wanted to go and wanted to stay.

He had me and I knew it. He must always have had no doubt that in this kind of showdown, he'd win. If it had been anyone else I had ever known—and I felt at the time I could say it of those I was yet to know—I would have said *Jump*, and gone back to bed. Carlos would have done it.

That night he and his incredible will had triumphed, and he had my attention until the sun came up and we both fell asleep on the couch in the living room.

"Meybe robbers."

OGDEN WAS A FORGOTTEN WORLD to us after the first month except when a letter from Lilly arrived. She wrote him wonderful letters, full of play and caring. As I read them with Carlos, I also hovered somewhere between not wanting him to go home and wanting him to have at least all that to go home to.

"Hello, Baby," one letter began. "I know you will smile when you see the word *baby* cause I made you *laugh* when I call you that. Hope you are all fine. Were o.k. I got your letter and Mama is very very happy to hear from you." Later in the letter she said, "The evenings are very long." I thought about that one, and about why I felt surprised he'd taken his "Hello, Baby!" home. Or had he brought it from there?

Somehow the letters all ended up being to both of us. One thing Lilly and I managed was to have our mutual love of the same boy be a tie, not a division. She signed her letters not Mrs. Salazar now, nor Lilly Salazar, but "I remain a friend always, Lilly." She did remain a friend to me always, and in later years, when Carlos was in and out of hospitals, she became one of my very good friends.

In looking back, I am amazed at how easy it was for me to fall into motherhood, however temporary. I loved cooking and caring for a boy of my own to the point of being almost a parody of a mother. I would sometimes set the table for breakfast immediately after dinner so that everything was handsomely ready for morning. Carlos thought this zeal hilarious, and he would go right to the table at 9:00 or 10:00 p.m., sit down, pick up his knife and fork and stand them at the ready on either side of his plate, waiting for what appeared to be forthcoming.

Carlos's language developed so quickly in these months that I could scarcely keep him in enough new experiences to accommodate his expanding abilities. A new bank had opened on the ground floor of our building, and it prompted me to think that one activity he didn't have a vocabulary for was saving money. So on a Friday night we cleaned up, got a little cash together, and went to dinner before going to the bank to open a savings account for him. What we had was indeed a new experience, one that left both of us deeply shaken.

Carlos was afraid of violence. I never knew him to be physically violent himself as a boy, although he could be emotionally rough, and he was terrific at provoking anger. Someone's violence, though, alarmed him more than any other thing. Once I took him and his classmates to visit the county jail in Ogden—I guess I saw it as an object lesson; I was surprised to find him trembling, arms flung about my legs like a terrified toddler, when a prisoner grabbed his bars and rattled them.

It was crime, the thing Carlos had seemed to escape, that interrupted our idyll. We had taken the elevator down to the mezzanine and walked the few feet to the Viennese restaurant. We had a particularly cheerful time ordering, of all things not Viennese, *coq au vin*. I taught Carlos to pronounce it. I wrote the phrase out which sometimes helped him to understand. I'm sure I wrote some bastardized thing like coke-o-van under the French, and then we ordered, and he repeated it smartly as we ate. By the time we finished, we were stuffed and pleased about it.

We sat back over tea, and I went through the process of our main endeavor, opening a savings account. When Carlos had the language for it down, he paid our bill, talking now at such moments rather than remaining mute and nervous. Then we walked down the corridor to the bank, which was always open Friday evenings.

We were just about to step up to the wicket, as everyone called it in Canada, when we looked up to see three hooded figures rush in. Everything fell at once into chaos. The biggest of the three carried a machine gun which he suddenly raised up over his head as he leaped into the air like a broad jumper and knocked in the gate that led back to the window and the money tills, and of course the safe.

The second man seemed to disappear, but he must have followed his athletic associate. The third man, who wasn't five feet from us, trembled horribly, a pistol wavering in his hand, and he stuttered over and over again, "Ge-get down, everybody, d-down. Get on the floor." All the while, he fumbled with the gun, apparently trying to flip it off safety. A frightened robber was far more alarming to me than one with conviction.

As Carlos and I got down on the cold marble floor, he gave me one of those all-knowing looks of his, full of awareness and steadiness, and sadness. In reflection, I can see that he was trying to give me courage as well. I lay beside him, an arm over his back. When I realized bullets might be fired, I climbed up over him and half covered his body. He was still so small. My thought at the time was that I couldn't let him be killed. I must have felt my trying to protect him would reassure him, but it probably scared the hell out of him. If I wanted him safe for his own sake and for mine, I desperately wanted to keep the boy Lilly had entrusted to me safe for her as well.

Suddenly a machine gun did rip into action. It seemed to split air and brain alike, and the silence that followed was full of a kind of collective, still insanity. It was forever before someone sat up and said, "They've gone, they've gone."

Carlos and I were out of the bank, in the elevator, and into our own apartment before the security guard could lock the doors and begin interrogating those present. When we were safely inside, I noticed Carlos looked blank. *That's real fear,* I thought, and I wondered what my own expression was.

Hearing ambulances, I led us out on the balcony and we watched five of them arrive. We pondered silently behind blanched faces how many people might have been wounded or killed. We didn't find out that none had been until the next morning.

Carlos slept on a makeshift cot in my room that night. In the following days, he crept about his business with a wary expression. If two or three men got on the elevator together, he would catch my eye and mouth when they weren't looking, "Meybe robbers."

Within two weeks our happy lives were changed by more than robbers.

"Mouse was very sad yes or no."

SPRING VACATION BEGAN on a raw day, wind slicing off the St. Lawrence and driving the chill factor down to -50°. Looking out over the city was a study in gray; the merest change was discernable between land and sky. The buildings, dark in their silhouettes, provided the only contrast. It would have been beautiful if you could have relinquished the longing to be outside, but going out into the arctic air was like taking a spear between the temples.

To occupy myself, I tried to devise a system of covering the balcony with a strip of plastic grass so I wouldn't have to take my dog in the elevator and down fifteen floors, then along two blocks, to get him to the park. I looked out the window at the smudgy, frozen city and decided to wait another day to take Carlos to Boston.

The second morning was worse than the first. The monochromes seemed to keep narrowing, and the usually lovely city flattened to monotony. The busses that sped along St. Mary's provided the only foreground color—a black stain over everything. Even if new snow fell, it grayed by the time it hit the ten-foot piles of darkened snow along the roadways.

That morning Carlos came to me with a note and the phone book. On the slip of paper he handed me were written two words, one above the other:

air
sister

He turned to the Yellow Pages and said, "Airport."

The atmosphere around me thinned as I found the long listing of airlines. He picked out United, the airline he had come to me on, and wrote down the telephone number beside the word *air*. Then he asked me to write my sister's phone number beside her name.

I wrote her telephone number down and then asked, "What for?" too full of feeling to use the extended speech I was trying to teach him.

"I will home in the morning," he said—said it with resignation and definition.

I made the call to the airport, got his suitcase down, moved through the tasks involved in sending him home. *It's best for him*, I told myself, realizing I hadn't begun to envision the future. My own attempts at stoicism annoyed me.

"When did you decide?" I asked later in the evening. What a question to come up with. I was sorry I'd asked it. "Never mind that," I added, but he was already responding.

"I don't know," he answered, and he probably didn't know what all called him back to Utah. He had been afraid in Montreal since the bank robbery. When men got on the elevator, he still mouthed silently to me, "Meybe theese." Everyone had become the Robber to him.

"Why do you want my sister's number?" I asked still later.

"If trouble, will with her to call you." He knew where she lived in Ogden, and this gave me a moment's bleak little comfort.

Carlos dressed in his school uniform for the flight home—gray slacks and blue blazer, now enlivened by the yellow Montreal Oral School for the Deaf patch which we'd stitched to the left pocket. He had on his blue-and-yellow tie and a rakish blue cap. As I looked at him, I figured in my mind what grade my own son would have been in.

When he was ready to go to the airport, he came into the bathroom where I was combing my hair. He perched up on the counter and sat silently, waiting for me to finish. As I completed my preparations—delays, really—he pulled me over to him, taking my face in his small hands. He gave me a long look, intent and graceful, and then he quite eloquently bent toward me and kissed me. It was a kiss full of fondness and friendship, of thanks and celebration. Montreal had been an island for both of us, and we knew outside words what it meant for ourselves and for each other.

The drive to the airport was the other side precisely of his arrival. In place of wild anticipation was stillness. We hardly spoke, we hardly stirred in our seats.

Finally we were there. He was outfitted with a halter, a number stretched between its straps so that he could be identified and met by a volunteer in Chicago. She would see that he transferred planes safely. Even as overwhelmed as Carlos looked with his number strapped over his coat, I thought how much of his little-boyness he had lost in the last months. My grand lad was becoming a young man and I hadn't noticed.

I asked a thousand questions about the dependability of the arrangements. What if there was a flight delay? Could volunteers be counted on for this sort of thing? What if no one showed up? Or he got sick? Or frightened? What if there was an emergency? Or if somehow they simply lost track of him? What if he changed his mind? What if he stayed on the plane in Chicago and didn't transfer and . . .

Finally I was certain that a stewardess would stay with him all the time, that his number would identify his next flight, and that someone would decidedly be there to lead him to a second plane that would carry him home.

And so I let him go.

I got into the car and drove to the nearest theater, went inside, bought a large buttered popcorn, and sat three times through *Madame X* with Lana Turner.

Spring came to the rest of the world before it came to Montreal that year. As winter slowly, almost imperceptibly, began to dissolve into itself, all its cast-offs were bared. I noticed that an odd record of the foregoing months had been kept in those dirty ten-foot drifts of snow. But they no more caught the essence of winter than someone's saved garbage would have. Not a trace of the white brilliance of January and Carlos's arrival lingered in the accumulation along the sidewalks of Earnscliffe and St. Mary's. Those days had become as ethereal as the bells of horses tinkling through the snows of another century.

Present, and all too real, was a smutted, littered metropolis. Its busses roared by relentlessly, spewing a trail of exhaust that fell over the already dingy snow until it looked like odd-shaped lumps of charcoal. Layered in it were the orange peels of December, the gum wrappers of January, half a sheet of homework from February. Worst of all were the contributions of a thousand dogs, perfectly preserved since as far back as November.

Life itself seemed too cold to move. Overnight my interest in the mix of newness, quaintness, and sophistication that had at first intrigued me felt like someone else's. What remained was the bracing against below-zero weather that extended into yet another week and the stiffening under a flat sky whose only change was from gray to black and back to gray again.

A letter from Lilly came in a couple of weeks. It was not in response to a letter of mine but certainly to a question in my heart. "No, I never was sorry Carlos went to visit you," she began. "Oh sure we missed him but I knew he was happy. I think he had the blue's he cried Wednesday night, said he was thinking of you's. I told him he could get to see you's again. Yes I am sure he like to visit you again."

She ended the letter with saying, "Carlos doesn't ever stay home."

Then a postcard, distinguished front and back and signed Mr. Carlos Louis Salazar, arrived and was put away. The message was brief:

> Dear Parker,
> Hello. Mouse was very sad yes or no. I miss you.
> Love Carlos. Mother says hello I love you.
> I was sad sometime.

In the next letter that arrived, Carlos included his own rendition of "Hello, Dolly!" I read through it standing out on the balcony above Montreal and picturing him in the yard of his blue house in Utah. When I came to the line, "Jeri will never go away again!" I was astonished at what he'd managed to make the song say.

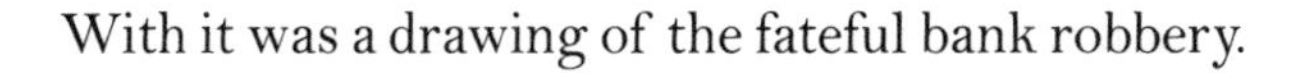

With it was a drawing of the fateful bank robbery.

April 1, 199

Dear Jeri Parker,
I love you very much.
I miss you, I give you
the picture. Love Louis

In early April another letter came. It began with a sad boy's face drawn at the top of the page and "I was sad" written over it. Diagonally up from it to both corners ran a line of XOXOXOXOXOXOXO.

> My Dear Parker,
> Hello Parker. I was very sad everyday. I was very cried sometime. Yesterday Ernie is car fast. I love you very much.
> This picture is for you to keep in your scrap book.
> Love, Love, Carlos

Four days later another letter arrived. This one began with a tic-tac-toe frame full of X's and O's. "Hello Parker" was written at an angle across the top margin:

> My Dearest Parker,
> This picture is for you to keep in your scrap book. I love you very much. I love you very much.
> I was very sad. I was very cry everyday. When go to Utah.
> Love, Love, Carlos

I changed my plans to move to Germany—I had been asked to teach there—and arranged to return to Utah.

"Momomom, I died."

"HE'S BEEN WAITING for yous," Lilly said when I drove up. "He wouldn't go nowhere all week. 'Jeri will come,' he told me," and she chuckled.

Then Carlos was standing in the doorway, sleepy-eyed and shirtless. He came over to me and leaned his rumpled head against my shoulder, reaching his arms around my waist.

"Too far," he murmured, and then to his mother, "Can go?" His speech as well as his language had taken a turn for the worse, but I had no trouble understanding him.

"If you want to," Lilly answered in her marvelous accent—the words strung along precisely; a metronome couldn't have gotten it better. Carlos disappeared behind a curtained doorway. When he returned, he had put a shirt on and was carrying a large brown paper bag half full of odds and ends he thought he might need.

"When should he be back?" I asked, wondering at the arrangement that seemed to work for everyone with virtually no talking about it.

"It don't matter," she said. "When he is ready."

He stayed two years, with frequent visits to Lilly and Patterson Avenue. I bought a house, and a dog for Carlos, and we settled into the foothills he'd once sought refuge in.

I suppose it is a great advantage that we can edit our memories. I have let mine of my life with Carlos in that house contract into a few while the brief time in Montreal continues to unfold in my mind. But I couldn't have guessed it would be that way at the time. We sat on the porch of our new home and laughed at the German shepherd Carlos named Parker Salazar. We dug out the old raft I'd stored and took half the neighborhood rowing on the reservoir. Marian was there a lot, and we had barbeques in the grape arbor.

But a new element emerged. Even though we had within us all the same buoyancy, not much that happened in those years was buoyant. At the bridge that spanned his youth and his manhood, Carlos had an accident that almost cost him his life. It would have been easy for me to prevent that accident, but that's not how it happened.

One Saturday afternoon I had dropped Carlos and his friend Corky at Rainbow Gardens, the big swimming pool at the mouth of the canyon. It was everyone's favorite, whatever state of restoration or deterioration it was in. It stayed cool in the canyon breeze and sat right down among the pines and scrub oak—you could see the trees from inside its clear, vaulted ceiling or go outside and wander through them. When you were out there, you got a wonderful blend of worlds, the smell of pines mixed with the smell of chlorine.

I liked leaving the boys that day and going downtown to have lunch with my very funny friend Ardith. I congratulated myself on letting Carlos be out on his own. I felt that I was doing things the way my grandmother would have—she didn't hover over her kids but let them grow up, and I knew it was time for me to let Carlos do that. I wasn't worried about it. The boys were both nearly fifteen and had spent a lot of time in swimming pools, and Corky was calm and steady, a good influence on Carlos and better than he was at making his way in the hearing world.

I returned to the pool in a little over an hour to pick them up but I couldn't find them. I knew something was wrong in those first seconds, and the recollection of sitting downtown laughing over lunch while whatever it was happened was unbearable to me. The pool area was heavily landscaped with potted palms, and I was scanning the water so intensely, I kept bumping into them. Backing away from one, I realized I was disoriented with fear. A man whose hands seemed to fly about his body told me I'd better get to Dee Hospital.

I looked out the window before me. I could see the road I'd come on winding up into the canyon; then it sagged suddenly. "Is he—? Should I —?" I felt as though power to some projector-like apparatus had been whacked off. It seemed to me as though I must not so much hurry as begin something.

I was trembling so violently on that drive to the hospital, my knees kept hitting the steering wheel. "Stay on Harrison Boulevard," I said aloud when I got to it. The sound of my voice let me keep taking the next step. "You're almost there—turn right on Twenty-fourth." I was still talking to myself when I saw the red brick of the hospital. I didn't so much park the car as just stop it and get out. I made myself not run; I very deliberately walked up the steps to the porch and the bronze-plated door. I knew the way to the emergency room; I didn't stop at the desk. A nurse followed me into the screened area of beds. "Carlos Salazar?" I asked. She pointed to an enclosure and I pulled back its curtain.

He lay limp and strangely colored, his lips sharply defined by the change. When he saw me, he tried to rise up on one elbow, but he sank back, holding out his twig-like arms. "Momomom, I died," he murmured, and I saw that a new kind of sadness had found him. Maybe it was awareness; they can look the same.

Little by little I learned that he had been found unconscious on the bottom of the swimming pool in a dark section where the blue paint had peeled. He would have been barely visible to his friend Corky, who pointed and cried out. Corky would have sounded different to others if he raised his voice in alarm—crazy, probably, and I wondered how a parent stands trying to gauge everything—what a child will be able to do in calm, what he'll do in an emergency. That's when I thought of Lilly and the call I would make to her.

Minutes must have gone by before Carlos was pulled from the dark spot. All the terminal signs of death had been present, but the lifeguard had performed mouth-to-mouth resuscitation. An ambulance was called when he didn't regain consciousness. I saw the ambulance fleeing along the streets I had just driven, and wondered if he had regained consciousness in there and lain listening to the wail of the siren.

The water in Carlos's lungs caused a severe case of pneumonia He was in an oxygen tent for a week, and the first of our many long talks in a hospital began. When he regained a little strength, we laughed about the possibility of his smoking and blowing himself directly into the next world, and we exchanged accounts of our days. But mostly we wrote each other letters, which would remain for us not only a means of trading information and affection, but also of fixing that information, tying it down. While he was in the hospital, I realized that I was not the only one who wondered what had been understood, what confused, in our exchanges.

As I watched him in those hours—half boy, half man—the old questions came back to my mind. Given his few, few advantages, where would his life take him? What qualities would win out in him?

The next thing that happened went through Carlos not like an accident but like a long sickness. One late autumn day, he was sitting on the front porch of our house when his dog, Parker Salazar, darted in front of a white speeding car. Carlos had been enraptured by Parker Salazar—he always called her by her full name. From his first look at her, he'd scarcely done anything but care for and admire her. He had even tried to master Serge's trick of feeding her a tube of dog food from a can. I don't know that Carlos even realized his dog had darted out into the street. I hope he didn't see the accident, but he saw the aftermath—his dog lying still, looking up at the sky in a great pool of blood. Her heart had been exploded by the impact.

It was probably as grotesque a thing as Carlos was ever to see. He ran almost crazed into the house to find me. When I came into the kitchen, he was pointing and crying out, "Park, Park." I couldn't understand him, and he became more and more frenzied, all the while shrieking "Mahka, Mahka" until he couldn't say it, and he took me by the hand, half angry at my slowness, and dragged me to the porch. One look and I knew he had been saying, "Parker, Parker," shortening the name of the dog for whom it was too late.

I sent him into the house and faced the street. When I came in from my grizzly task, Carlos was lying under a rocking chair. He didn't come out until it was time to go to bed. When I woke the next morning, he was sleeping on the floor beside my bed.

He didn't talk about his dog again. A year later when I asked him if he would like another dog, he said simply, "No, meybe she be hit." As far as I know, he never had another dog.

"I will wife you."

HOW TIME MARKS ITSELF has always been curious to me. Where Carlos was involved, it was by springs. It was 1970; he was halfway to his seventeenth birthday. As the second April on Pierce Avenue drew to a close, he picked up his schoolbooks, came into the kitchen where I was, and said, "I'm going home." When I looked up, he was gone, as softly and quietly as memory goes.

Nothing that preceded his leaving had been soft and quiet. And nothing that followed was. He was right to leave, although at the time I would have changed any of it if I could have—the timing, the way, certainly the fact itself.

Through the rest of that year, I thought of him walking down my sidewalk for the last time, not even taking a half-full brown paper bag with him. What did he walk home to? What did he close a door against? After all the words, I'd never imagined that, as with the rest of us, Carlos could learn to speak and then prefer silence.

If I'd felt hollowed when he left Montreal, I felt rearranged now, as though he'd been lifted from my cells. I didn't think about him much in the first days—it was all feeling. And I was tired; all I wanted was to lie down. Once in a while I wondered if he'd had dinner, if one of his brothers had taken his bedroom. I called Lilly, and she said no more about his returning than she had about his leaving.

A hymn kept running through my mind, "Rest, rest for the weary soul; Rest, rest for the aching head." That was what we both needed now. "Rest, rest, oh, ye weary, rest."

The first movie I'd seen came back to me. I was a little girl with my mother, and I wasn't fooled. I knew that all the horses and all the men and the children and the women were waiting backstage to come on for their scene. I'd asked Mother how they got it to go so smoothly. Nothing ever seemed to happen out of order, as it did for me now.

Perhaps exhaustion itself made me able finally to let the last scenes with Carlos come back once more, almost as though I could take them into my hands and then let go of them. Bit by bit, the incomprehensible sorted itself out.

Everything had become an unexpected tangle, or so it had seemed. But now a prelude emerged to my dark-haired young man full of gentle ways leaving his boyhood affection for me and crossing into a sulky passion. He'd slammed around in a hard possessiveness, and I'd been bewildered by this most inexplicable of all his faces. Or had I?

In the winter he brought home a picture of a girl and showed it to me. "Margaret?" I asked, recognizing her as one of his school playmates. I looked again. She had become a teenager.

Carlos turned the picture over in his hands, and I read:

> To Carlos
> I love you, Margaret

I felt him watching me closely. I was watching as well. Surely I wasn't going to be jealous of his entering into the world of girlfriends? Then he said the line he was to repeat like a litany in the next months, "Why you too old?"

Another shift preceded his leaving. We had been watching *Room at the Top* on television late one night. I had been lying on the couch, and Carlos had been trying to sneak up beside me. I'd laughed and poked at him, playfully trying to beat him back to the floor. In one of his sudden reversals of mood, he became angry. When I tried to cajole him out of it, he went to his room and closed the door. I heard him lock it and, a few minutes later, unlock it.

It was one of the thousand versions of the old, old standoff—his wanting to sleep with me, my refusing to let him. The unaccountable fatigue had begun then. Finally I was tired in my soul. The easy answers of yesteryear sprang away from me. When I tried to ignore him and go back to watching the film that had been so compelling when I'd seen it a few years earlier, I was jumpy and touchy myself, and I wasn't sure I wanted to see how bad life would get for the characters being played by Simone Signoret and Laurence Harvey. My resilience, I couldn't help noticing even then, wasn't worth much more than what Carlos could muster.

A new loneliness was present in those days of puzzling over what was best for Carlos, best for both of us. It wasn't as easy to gallop around together with him sixteen and me thirty. And always the question lay at the back of my mind—what will become of him?

He was still angry when I went to my room. I could feel it through the door. And I was at the mercy of that swallowing fatigue. I fell into a strange sleep almost as soon as I got into bed. I had the feeling that the dream I dreamed that night was there waiting for me, as tangible as my pillow and blankets. Within it was someone, a man with sad, wise eyes and a finely made face. He knew me, and his melancholy eyes gladdened when he saw me. I didn't know him at first, although he was familiar to me. Then I recognized that it was Carlos, not as the boy I had just looked in on, but Carlos my age. It was odd, I remember thinking, that I was not astonished.

He touched my hair, my cheek, as if to assure me he was real. A great reaching comfort spread through me. To have him by my side for a moment, not as a rampaging, puzzling boy but as a man—there was a kind of luxury and peace in it that was unknown to me.

As I smiled at his coming, he put his arms around me and held me. Everything was marked by a slowness and richness that struck me as not of this world. There was nothing young in his embrace, but for an instant I remembered him as a boy and a nameless sorrow took me. Is this, I wondered, what would have been in another time, another place?

The moment the thought came to me, it *was* that other time, other place, and his fine mouth kissed my cheek, the mere side of my mouth. He looked at me as he had done when he left Montreal, a long look before the unutterable greeting of each other in a far, dear world. I held and was held by everything that mattered to me—friend, counselor, consoler, gladdener. Son was not among the things he was to me at that moment.

Finally I got up and went into the living room and then the kitchen, wanting the comfort of chairs, cabinets, dishes. A note stood against one of the cups I had set out for breakfast. I read it, and for the second time because of Carlos, I put my head in my hands and wept. His brief message fell over me like fate. There in his familiar hand were the words, "I will wife you."

"Nothing want."

MANY YEARS PASSED before it seemed quite natural to me that Carlos and I should have been a little in love with each other for a time. But eventually I came to see that, like so many before us, we were destined to lose our hearts to our pygmalions. If he was in some ways my creation—certainly he bore my imprint where language was concerned—I was as much marked by his shaping. And no shaping is so deep, I had found, as that tied to how we are able to express ourselves and how we are able to be understood.

But such philosophical considerations were not comforting at the moment; in fact, they were not even possible. In time they were. I admired the efficiency that had let Carlos gather himself together and go home. Wasn't this separation a gift of strength rather than a weak retreat? Would I have had him cling to me into manhood rather than stride from that possibility any way he could?

And I came to understand why he'd said, when I'd asked him if he wanted me to bring his belongings to him, "Nothing want." As I packed away his blue blazer and ice skates along with shirts and vests and pants and caps and suits and Boy Scout knives and binoculars and taws, I remembered again the brown paper bag he'd brought from his home when he'd come to live with me. In it had been a pair of socks and two pairs of shorts. He had his shirt on, he'd explained. I realized with dismay that I'd heightened the contrast between his two worlds with my indulgences.

Of course he didn't want to trundle gold Neruda jackets to the neighborhood where at the moment the style was closer to stowaway than cutting edge. If I thought about it, it was a style I preferred myself.

Trying to learn from him, I looked to my own life.

"I am real happy to leave school."

ACROSS TOWN from my adjustment, Carlos flung himself into his return to the stucco house beside the overpass. Its turquoise paint was now chipped and faded, and many of the boys and girls who had played there when I first came were gone. Some were already married. A few were at the Raft, Ogden's correctional institution for young lawbreakers. Several had gone to California or New Mexico to work.

Those who remained were in their tough years. Carlos loved them overnight. He went from being meticulous to being not just unkempt but slovenly. He gave up haircuts—tongue cannot tell how exact they had had to be. He appeared to give up soap and toothpaste as well. His too-big dirty shirt was always half unbuttoned. The more ripped and torn something was, the better it suited him. And his attentive manner fell away. He tossed his head arrogantly, held his mouth in a half-open jeer. He became loud and rude.

None of this stood for much in my reckoning. What did was that he became unmistakably mean. He seemed to like nothing better than to start a fight. I hoped for the first months after he left that he was enjoying a fashionable quarrel with the world, like everyone else in his generation. I gave up that hope when he sent a letter to Marian, who was living in Europe. "I was hate," he wrote. "I was hate, hate, hate."

By then I had met the man I'll call David, and I was unreasonably happy. I had moved to Salt Lake City and was absorbed in him and in my work. I was doing research and teaching a few classes at the university. When summer came, I was in southern France or Beirut, sometimes as a tour guide. Wherever I was, if there was a river, I'd meet David when I could, and we'd stand beside each other and cast upstream.

Fragmentary accounts of the life Carlos was leading continued to find their way to me. I never had the heart to seek them; in fact, I usually cut them short. They were invariably bitter accounts, given by teachers who had grown beyond any fascination they might once have felt for beautiful Carlos. But occasionally one of his former friends, outraged or worried by him, would come to me to talk, and I would listen.

Whoever it was doing the reporting, I noticed where Carlos was concerned, everyone was ready to make the too-easy journey from assumption to accusation, and on without a hitch to condemnation. At least I'll avoid that, I told myself, as random details accumulated. He was said to have stolen cars, to have deluded cunningly and in contemptible ways his young girlfriends, to have lived in a freight car for half a year, to have stood by the river and thrown rocks at an old couple. He told me himself many years later that he had seen something happening across the river and then there was a dead baby. More and more people called him "that little foreigner" and they would add, "What else could you expect?"

"He's not a foreigner," I answered to that one, answered it with a little too much vigor, remembering a loving boy with elegant ways.

I continued to talk to Lilly on the phone from time to time, when she had a phone. "He don't seem happy," she reported. Usually she said, "Don't ask me about that kid, I don't know what he's doing. I'm so mad at him I could kill him, you know." But at times she initiated the discussion of him. "He don't stay here much. Him and Ernie don't get along," she told me. "I don't know what to do with him. He's had trouble with the police too."

One day over a year after Carlos had returned to Patterson Avenue, I looked out the window of my study to see a wisp of a boy-man dismount from an enormous motorcycle. If I hadn't been so amazed to see Carlos Salazar in my driveway, I'd have stood there laughing at the little body trying to get off of the Harley Davidson without having it crush him. He'd barely grown since he'd gone home, and he was thinner than he'd ever been. His hair had become a mad tangle that ended below his shoulders. As he came up to me, I saw that he had his first hopes of a beard. Nothing remained of the waif charm that had been so irresistible in him. His new swagger was unconvincing, unbecoming. And it was somehow incongruous in someone so small.

"Found you," he said to me. "Why Salt Lake City? Never home."

"I'm not home much, that's true," I answered.

"That's true," he said.

"Is that your bike?"

"No, friend," he replied. The toss of his head came. "Stole."

One thing I had no inclination to do was indulge his excitement in recounting his misadventures. Instead of pursuing the subject, I fell back on trying to feed him, but this time he accepted only a Coke. He looked unwell and fell asleep on the couch after talking for a few minutes. I let him sleep, still amazed to get a look at and to hear a few words from the phantom Carlos.

When he awoke, he laughed off having fallen asleep. "Party last night. I was drink too much. Too many women." He got himself up and reached for his key.

"Will come," he said on the porch, and he walked over and put his thin arms around me and bent his matted head against mine for a moment.

As he walked to his bike, the whole of him danced before me. His intelligence, his deep caring, his profound connection to life would extend beyond this period of furious searching, I was sure. For the first time in a long while, my thoughts of Carlos were full of hope. He couldn't have seen it in my eyes; the Harley Davidson took all he had. A backward glance would have been death, given his wheelie exit.

Carlos stopped by once in a while after that. The visits never changed much, except that as they became more frequent, he seemed to more easily find moments of respite from his bravado. He tossed himself around with a little less importance. He talked about his life in broader terms than what he intended as criminal boasting. He asked about my life. He thought it was colossally stupid of me to have moved to Salt Lake City and become involved with the university, he made that clear, but he asked me innumerable questions about it. We were working at understanding each other's new worlds, I knew that.

He showed me a picture of his girlfriend on one visit. I asked about her—was she deaf?

"No, hearing," Carlos told me. "Hearing high school."

"She looks nice," I said. This was not the part of Carlos's life that worried me, and when he saw that, he added, "But never happy. Fight, fight, fight."

"They have him on those tranquilizers at school," Lilly told me once when I called. I investigated. It was true—he was sedated at school, and he had been moved from the Oral Department to the Simultaneous Department, the signing and speaking option. In it, he now did little more than sign.

I wondered if, as he narrowed his world, he felt his great expectations slowly dwindle. A few years hence and he would not be a candidate for Gallaudet College, where he had talked of going with his deaf friends. Nor would he be accepted at the fine trade college for the deaf in Seattle. Meanwhile, he was getting less and less vocational training in his last years of school, and his speech and language skills continued to decline until he was hard even for me to understand.

None of us knew the battle Carlos was fighting in those days. We simply stood by and watched him go downhill and believed him when he bragged of drinking too much.

I heard from someone a few months later that Carlos was a father. A tiny Carlos somewhere in the world held my attention like few things had since I'd first seen him leaping and cavorting in the sunflowers. I had an overwhelming desire to find the baby and be sure he had everything he needed. From the first moment I learned that Carlos's girlfriend, still in high school, had had the child, I wondered whether she wanted him. Although Marian was back in Utah, I hadn't seen her for a long time, but I called her and told her that Carlos might have a son. Sensing what was in my mind, she said, "Don't go see that baby, Jeri."

Seven years later, the girl who had had the child would walk into Carlos's hospital room and present him with a photograph of his son, Charlie Salazar. He was a ringer for Carlos.

When I saw Carlos after I'd heard he had a baby, I wondered if I wanted to ask him about it. But by then he had his wallet out and was reaching into a crevice to drag forth a tiny, crumpled photo of a curly-headed fellow. He handed it to me with the words, "My son, Charlie." I admired him considerably for some time and then returned the picture. "No, for you," he insisted. When Carlos came almost to live in a hospital himself and visitors asked if the large, color photograph by his bedside was him as a boy, he always answered, "My son, Charlie."

The next thing I remember knowing about Carlos was that he was graduating from the School for the Deaf. I heard about it late, and had plans to be out of town that weekend. I was meeting David; it wasn't a plan I could easily change. And at any rate the time when I'd have thrown over anything to be part of what mattered to Carlos was behind me. Now my own imperatives kept me from being with him. I don't think Marian was there either.

A handful of years later, Carlos asked me why I hadn't come to his graduation. It was for me one of many reckonings with how much I'd misjudged what mattered to him. That I could miss his graduation always remained a puzzlement and a heartache to him. I'd have wagered at the time that he hadn't noticed.

The only other graduate that May 20, 1974, was Carlos's friend, Terry. Both of them gave talks. Carlos delivered his in fear and trembling, I was later told. It was a mix of his own hopes and thoughts and the highmindedness and grammar imposed upon him by his teachers. Almost the only sentence that was pure Carlos was, "I am real happy to leave school." I knew the "and go out to meet the world" wasn't his phrase.

For all his years of work in speech and language, almost no one in the audience could understand him as he read his hybrid talk. He was anything but the pride of the school.

Whatever the nature of his performance, I am deeply sorry I wasn't in the audience for his grand hour—to see him in the ruffled shirt and tuxedo he wore and to hear what he had to say. When he was almost thirty and had forgiven me for not being there, he gave me the program that contained his speech:

"My Graduation Time"

Today I feel a little bit like President Johnson when he said, "yesterday is not ours to recover, but tomorrow is ours to lose." He is gone now, but this message still leaves us this good advice. In my past school years I was wrong in many of the things I did. It seems that "trouble" was one of my companions. Perhaps with the tomorrow that is now here, I will find a way to be sure to always do things that are good. I must be a hard worker in whatever I do. I must accept the encouragement and the advice of good people.

Now that school has ended for me here at the Utah School for the Deaf I will have to go out and try to find a job. I have learned many things here that should help me, such as woodwork, some printing, and work in preparing our yearbook for printing. I have learned to read and write, and most importantly, I have learned that I must live in harmony with all people.

"Tomorrow is ours to win or lose." If I want to win the very best, I should try to someday go to Seattle Community College in Washington. There I could learn more about the work I want to do. The training I would receive there would help me "win" higher wages to live on.

I thank all of the teachers, friends and others who have helped me for this day of graduation. Your help and the many years I have been in school now brings me a very great reward. I am real happy to leave school and go out to meet the world. My tomorrow is here and it is up to me whether I "win or lose."

Thank you.
Carlos Salazar

"I was almost dead."

DURING THE YEARS that Carlos was peripheral to my life, I was out of the state and out of the country often. I didn't keep track of how much time went by between getting bits of information about him. Occasionally I'd call Lilly. I can't remember who told me he'd had a baby, but it wasn't her, and I assumed this was a second baby, not Charlie. That there were babies of his in the world was of enormous import to me, and again I had to suppress the protectiveness I'd felt for him. I thought of Roethke's line in "Elegy for Jane." I too had "no rights in this matter," although there wasn't a death here. I was sorry the word *elegy* had come to mind.

Marian called to tell me she thought Carlos had gotten married. When I was in Ogden, I stopped by Lilly's. Yes, he was married, she said. She didn't seem tickled about it. "He had a boy," she added, and I recognized that that was what bothered her. But why? Something far less conventional than the old shotgun business would have to be afoot to throw Lilly.

I asked if he'd married his girlfriend from a few years back. "Oh, no!" she exclaimed. The contrast in possibilities seemed to make her more content with the present situation. "Those two don't even speak. And Carlos can't see that boy. He almost went to jail over that."

I was confused. "Is that the child he has?" I asked her.

"Charlie Salazar is his. But like I say, he can't see him."

"Were they married?" I asked, surprised at Charlie's last name.

"No. Carlos wouldn't."

"Why is Charlie's name Salazar?" I continued. As soon as I said it, I realized how fully stupid it was.

She looked at me. She was sizing up my intellect as well. "Carlos is the father," she answered. Her speech hadn't lost any of its clip, its lilt.

"He has a telephone," she told me as I left. "He don't live far from here." Her wanting me to see him led me to drive by the little house ten or fifteen blocks up the street from hers. It was a fetching place, neatly trimmed and as tidy as Carlos had been in his early years. There was no sign of life around the house, no car, no window open, and no one answered when I knocked repeatedly.

Marian had his phone number so she called Carlos's house later in the week and spoke with his wife. Her name was Linda, and she was anything but bashful.

"I need a crib," she said, "if you're getting something for the baby."

Marian called me at once. "Come on up here. We've got an order in for a baby present." So there were two babies—that took care of some of my confusion.

"We're a couple of pushovers," she said on the way to deliver the light green crib Linda had told us she preferred. We were both a bit chagrined at ourselves for falling right in with her wishes. "Well, it is Carlos's baby," we repeated, realizing that in all the years of our indulgences of him, he had never asked us for anything.

"How old is Carlos now?"

"He's twenty-three," Marian said in her precise voice. "He was born in 1953. That's advanced mathematics for you, isn't it?"

"Almost," I answered. "How did he get from ten to twenty-three?"

"He went to bed every night—well, most nights—and got up every morning like the rest of us."

As we drove up in front of the house, Carlos walked over to our car from the one he had been working on with his friends. It was a dry, hot summer day and he had his shirt off. He didn't look so thin when more than his arms came into view. He had wide shoulders and a broad, well-developed chest. He went to Marian's side of the car and opened the door for her. She got out and without a word they put their arms around each other. I couldn't see him, but I could see her smiling, trying not to rock back and forth with him. He looked like a tiny brown Atlas from the back. Then he came over to me.

The moment his eyes met mine, I knew the raucousness and mischief of his recent years—the tough days of ripped-up shirts, of alarming rudeness, of hair flowing like a wild mane halfway down his back—were behind him. But something more was missing, and I paid attention. His vitality, his stamina was gone.

His eyes had become sorrowful, and wise. I don't know why you could see it, but you could. His manner was that of the little boy he had been, all affection and tenderness and solicitation. When he put his arms around me, I took the chance to close my own eyes and bury them for a minute in his still-wild hair. I wondered how he'd stepped beyond anger, the main ingredient of his lost years.

Marian and I were absorbed in our separate thoughts as we drove away. Then I said, "Linda was easy enough to meet."

"She's bored," Marian answered. "We were a variation in her day."

"Something's wrong with him," I finally said.

"It isn't his baby, for one thing," Marian said. "It's pretty clear the father was black."

I had wondered, but I wanted terribly for Carlos to have a son he could raise. "No, it's got to be his. It's a little dark Salazar," I said.

"Carlos isn't the father. There is the opposite of resemblance. The baby doesn't look like Carlos or Lilly or any of the others—Robert, Miranda, Ernie. It isn't his baby." Marian was mad.

"You think he's been duped, don't you?" I said. "Don't worry. You're who taught me he always knows everything."

"I don't think he is well," I added some time later. "He looks gray." *He knows he is going to die* was what I thought to myself, and with a jolt, I realized that his father was dead at his age.

"Carlos isn't well, is he?" I asked Lilly as soon as I could reach her. I asked her who his doctor was. She wasn't sure. He'd been to several; she didn't know whom I could call.

I paid attention to time now. After a few weeks, I went to see him again. I struggled into his house with sacks of groceries for Thanksgiving and found him lying on the couch, a blanket covering him. The television droned across the room, which was darkened and overheated. He didn't get up, but I could hear him from the kitchen as I put things away, "Thank you very much. That's too much."

When I came back into the living room, he was asleep. I sat down at the end of the couch and tickled a foot, but there was no jolting him into life. He woke slowly, as though drugged.

I went straight to Lilly's from his place. "What's wrong with Carlos?" I asked. "He looks worse."

"He was in the hospital," she said. "They let him go, but he was so dizzy at home, they put him in an ambulance and sent him to one of those old folks' places in Salt Lake. He said to me, 'Find Jeri' but I didn't know how. He just kept saying, 'Find Jeri. I was almost dead.'" Lilly wouldn't have known how to reach me at the cabin, and she might have been too overwhelmed to try my Salt Lake City number.

"A nursing home? Why?" I asked.

"I don't know." Then she looked up with an idea. "Do you think they thought about a stroke? But he's too young." I'd forgotten how she could say those things. Lilly had changed with the years. She was heavier and graying. She looked older than she was. She'd had a hard life.

"Who can I call to find out more about Carlos?" I asked Lilly. I was furious with myself for my negligence.

"I don't know," she answered. "I try to talk to the doctors, but they won't tell me nothing. Once they told me he won't live a year."

So he'd gone in an ambulance to Salt Lake City, murmuring "Find Jeri." He'd spent two weeks alone—a young man who still looked like a boy—among old, maybe mindless people. He must have wondered why I didn't come. For myself, I wondered if he knew why he had been taken there. I never learned what his symptoms were beyond being dizzy or what testing had been done, what the results were. In a later conversation, Lilly said again, "Maybe he did have a stroke."

PART THREE

"I asked Lilly find you."

THE NEXT WORD I HAD of Carlos came while I was in Idaho's Centennial Mountains spending a month at my cabin. I didn't have to be there very long before I hardly knew a world existed outside the stand of pines surrounding the simple structure with its deck looking out into the forest and its walls of rough-cut Douglas fir the color of honey. It could even take my mind off Carlos.

Then one morning in about the middle of my stay, I drove to Pond's Lodge for groceries and mail. It was one of the few remaining grand structures up there; it had been carefully built and then rebuilt after a fire, its beams hewn of the same fir I loved. Every window and doorway was trimmed by hand in split pine. An old stuffed bear stood at the entrance of its massive lobby. We'd had strict orders as children to keep our hands off that bear, but he didn't look as if we'd spared him. I had worked as a waitress at Pond's Lodge one summer, and I'd at least kept him dusted, giving him a different name on every occasion—Brian, Hudson, Roger.

The lobby had been divided up over the years. You could trace the eras through those additions. A soda fountain was built in the fifties when we were all watching *I Love Lucy*. I'd run the fountain until Charlie Pond told me I was eating the profits and converted it to a bar. A dance hall was added in the sixties when the song "Wild Mary" yanked us out of our seats. A post office was squeezed in. There was always a grocery store, its walls lined with Norman Rockwell prints. A tackle shop got set up in time for *A River Runs Through It*.

a thousand voices

I noticed my name on the message board next to the grocery section as soon as I came into the lodge. One of my former students was behind the counter. I could tell from the tightness in her face that the message would change my life. I remember the shift in my body—from blithe and sun-baked to cold, inside and out. I had already lost the tranquility of my alpine days by the time she handed me a piece of folded notepaper. I seemed to take it in all at once rather than read it. I was on a plane to Salt Lake City an hour later. It never crossed my mind to drive. Or to spend time driving.

The facts in the message couldn't have been more straightforward:

> Jeri Parker 8-1-77
> Please call Lilly
> Carlos Salazar is in the hospital
> Needs kidney transplant. May have
> less than 6 mos. to live.

I had a dog up there and all I could think was how can I fly this dog home with me? It took me the full hour to find a friend to keep her, round up a few things, and make a dash for the airport in West Yellowstone. I knew the plane schedules and the fellow that handled Western Airlines flights. I flew out of that airport often to get to where David was, but I usually had time to make arrangements for my dog. "This trip isn't for luxury, is it?" my friend said and I nodded at his understanding.

I boarded the airplane, my head fizzing, my knees wobbly. Carlos came back to me with such force it was disorienting. His primacy in my life was never far below the surface. Once the plane took off, my bones, the vertebrae in my spine, became free of one another, lifting away to some place outside the body and the bondage of apprehension. I floated in the plane that floated in the ice-blue sky outside the window. I could have been a cloud. The forest was dark below, more brown than green. It was the color you'd get if you put a lot of alizarin in thalo green. Then the trees ended in a line—the timberline, which had always fascinated me—and farmland began. I felt the familiar ache to be back with the trees when we crossed that line. A faint mist blurred the patchwork of farms below. It was make-believe down there, I could see that, and I derived some comfort from the thought.

I was still in a kind of psychological checkout when the plane landed. As it touched ground, all the realities slammed back into me.

Carlos lay in Room 632 of the University Hospital like a bearded emperor, his hair spread black and limp against the white pillowcase, his dark eyes dulled from fever. From the look he gave me as I came into the room, I could see he had gone into his own world, beyond acceptance or despair.

"I asked Lilly find you," he said. His breathing was heavy and raspy. He tossed in his bed, half delirious, his body damp and hot, and there was the unceasing nausea. He lay stiff and lifted my hand to his face. "Forest," he said. So he could smell that life—pitch and pine and sage and grasses. I knew he was remembering it.

Finally he fell asleep, breathing against my fingers, but whenever I stirred to go, he woke and mumbled, "With me. One time with me." Close as he was to death that night, he roused himself whenever he could and murmured, "With me."

"I'm here," I answered, and it was enough. It was more than enough—it was at last abundance. After that, we returned as easily as children to the spontaneous affection that had defined our first years of knowing each other. "You same crazy," he said to me, "Same stay."

As I drove the rental car I'd picked up at the airport to my home that morning, I thought how at best we only know one another in fragments which, from unexpected time to time, fuse into a present whole. Time and place, how we misunderstand them, accuse them. I saw that what I might have taken for a few colored threads at one point in my life had become over the years the bright weave of continuity. Carlos, who had seemed to drop in and out of my life at random, was of course one of its central designs.

I don't remember what we talked about during the week that I stayed in Salt Lake City other than his condition, which I went over and over with him. Between my endless questions—the only sure way I had of determining what he knew—he was sick and sank back onto his bed. To see him eat, or try to, was agony. He would be perky in the morning, eager for breakfast to arrive. When it came, he would sit up for it like a neat kitten, paying fastidious attention to the little details of preparation. He would shake out his napkin, tuck it up under his chin, and line up his silverware to his satisfaction. Then he would reach for a piece of bacon, take a respectable bite of it, and gesture for me to hand him his basin—all almost in one motion. As many times as I watched the process, I never saw him anticipate the sickness that followed the moment he tried to eat.

"For how long?" I asked.

"Almost three year."

"The same? That fast? Every time you eat?"

"For one year," he answered.

Where had I been? He was in renal failure, why hadn't I seen that? And why couldn't I find out anything about a possible stroke? Were they linked? My inquiries had never led anywhere and I'd stepped back, thinking it wasn't my place to push. In reflection, I see that I'd left more to Lilly than Lilly could handle. And I would have to say that I was genuinely surprised that Carlos had said, "I asked Lilly find you."

"All my life?"

"A DECISION MUST BE MADE, is that right?" I said to Carlos's doctor the next day.

"Yes, and you can be helpful to us."

"What does it look like?" I asked.

"What is your relationship to the family?" he responded.

"We're friends, good friends."

"Will they look to what you think in the decision?"

"Maybe. I think so." I wondered why he'd asked.

"Carlos came to my office about three years ago," he told me. "He had a history of being socially . . . how shall I say this? He was not much benefit to anyone at that time. We have to make decisions every day about what happens to someone like Carlos. Here was a deaf boy, who had been in and out of jail, was on welfare, couldn't hold a job. And his kidneys were failing. Frankly, we sent him back home to let nature take its course. He was not told of alternatives, of dialysis, for example."

Not ever told? Not informed? I was furious. I had a hard time not saying to him *Who do you think you are?* I was distraught with myself as well.

For a long time, Carlos and I had moved in circles that rarely intersected, but how had I forgotten his vulnerabilities, his limitations? Then I offered myself some respite. Extend a little mercy, I sat there thinking, and see that what you have here is what lasts.

As the doctor continued his explanations—if that is what they were—I thought of the Carlos I knew. I could see his head coming up through the yellow petals of the sunflowers on Patterson Avenue, could see him wearing his oversized blue coat with the picture he'd drawn of

Deaf Carlos pinned to his back, could remember my first look at Wow very POW—his expression as he handed the drawing to me bearing no small resemblance to the baby bird. I remembered his tramping alongside me in the forest I had just left. And that other side of him—for the first time I smiled at the memory of his trying to stay upright on his Harley Davidson. What did this man know or wonder of the range and heart and daring of Carlos Salazar?

The doctor took out a pipe and made a little show of emptying it, filling it, tamping it. He was no stranger to arrogance. He clearly assumed that his own rituals were of interest. He lit the pipe as a saint might light a taper. The voice continued after he'd luxuriated in a few puffs. "Then Carlos came back last week. His history had changed. He was married, had a son—although it is unlikely that it is his."

I tried to think how Carlos would see this man and how I could respond to him with my failing lad's best interests in mind. "Why do you say that?" I asked.

"By that time he probably was sterile from the medications he was taking."

"Is that a permanent condition? And would those medications affect a baby—a fetus?"

"Yes. We'd have to abort a pregnancy. Eventually potency goes too." He drew on his pipe again and leaned back to expel the smoke. "Well, Carlos came with a job, a wife, a son. And he was dying. He would have been dead in six days if he hadn't gotten in here. And it's hard when you get right down to that week."

He had let Carlos get right down to that week. I disdained him, but I allowed him a little ground for having reconsidered Carlos's fate. My boy, I knew, wouldn't grant any respect to an arch and controlling man like this. That probably wasn't in his favor.

"What we're doing now is dialyzing him. You've seen the shunt in his foot we put in before you got here. The dialysis is performed through it. Do you understand what dialysis is?" I said something about it doing the work of the kidneys, cleansing the blood. "Precisely," he answered. "You don't need to know more, except that the patient lives in a state of chronic uremia. In the hours after dialysis, some people are tired, or even sick. Then they feel good for a day. By the time they're back to dialysis, usually the next day, they're feeling the effects of the toxic build-up—sluggishness, sometimes nausea." He seemed to come to life in these details, using his pipe to make an inclusive sweep, an emphatic gesture. He went on for a long time about fistulas, antigen matches, chemistries, donors, all worked in between puffs of smoke blown ceremoniously into the air between us.

"What is the future for him on dialysis?" I asked. I wondered how Carlos would have handled the conversation. He would never have dealt in this many words. What an encumbrance we can make of them. For Carlos, I was sure it came down simply to was it tolerable or wasn't it?

"Frankly, I don't think Carlos has much of a future on dialysis. It takes two, probably four hours a day, three times a week. It's not a cure-all even then. The treatment slowly destroys cells in the blood, greatly lowering the patient's energy level. And there is a certain quality to it. It is grotesque in its way." There wasn't a lot of pipe activity here. "You always know you are the captive of that machine. Some people can adjust very well. But it takes enormous ability to comply. *Enormous* compliance. Carlos doesn't show any such ability. Until you came, we couldn't even get a blood sample without four assistants holding him down."

"You seemed like marauders to him. I don't think he understood anything of what was happening."

"That's his problem, isn't it?" He sat back in his chair.

"By no means just *his* problem," I said with real edge. Then I stopped myself, realizing I could be a factor in this man's decisions.

I disliked the doctor so much he seemed to me to have caused the problem. Perhaps he simply loves kidneys, their function, their malfunction, I told myself, trying not to respond in anger. "It doesn't sound like much of a life," I said. "And the alternative to dialysis is a transplant?"

"No. There is another. Death is an alternative."

"Do some people choose it?"

"Once in a great while. Or at least they think they've chosen it. Then suddenly they're dying and they're screaming, 'Help me, save me.' Not very many can go through with it." He said it with a cold shrug that was close to contempt.

It won't do Carlos any good if you sit here making assumptions about this man—you don't know very much about him yet. Don't do what he's doing. But however I looked at it, I couldn't put out of my mind the fact that he didn't know anything about Carlos.

"A donor has to be found for a transplant?" I asked.

He went into a lengthy discourse on live donors, cadaver donors. He swiveled in his chair. Then he asked me if I thought any of the Salazar family would give a kidney.

"Robert has said he would. So has Miranda. But they..." When I looked up, it was to look squarely at him, large in his chair across the desk from me. "Would you give away a kidney?"

"Let's put it this way. To a son I might, although I would wrestle with it. If something happened to my other kidney, I'd be Carlos in that bed down the hall. It's as simple as that. To a father, I wouldn't. I'd figure, 'You've had your years. I'm not going to jeopardize mine.'"

"But for another young person to give away a kidney?" I thought of Robert's instant generosity and my own reluctance—did he fully know what it would mean for him? What would Carlos's reservations be?

"What are the risks to Carlos if he has a transplant?"

There was the "Let's put it this way" again, followed by predictions—three years, perhaps six or seven—not more for Carlos with his high blood pressure—if it works, and then the increased susceptibilities—pneumonia, cancer, diabetes. And the weight gain, the puffiness, perhaps a hunched back. He would be in and out of hospitals, almost daily, after at least a six-week stay. Then weekly for a year, with rehospitalizations likely. "This is still new stuff," he said.

It was new stuff. It doesn't matter what comes along—when it is new, it's overwhelming. The kidney transplant procedure is refined now, and not that uncommon, but then it was like stepping off the edge of the world. It was even seen as an ethical dilemma—*should* you harvest a kidney? Harbor someone else's? It was, if not as shocking as cloning, very close.

So his beauty would go, I thought. His freewheeling style had already gone. And what would remain?

I ended with telling the doctor Robert was not Carlos's full brother. He chuckled. "There's a man upstairs," he told me. "We do blood types on all this. We know all about family history by the time we're through. This man upstairs is the son and heir—the *only* son and heir—of a prominent and wealthy Mormon family. They want that boy alive at any cost. Of course we don't tell the father, 'He isn't even your son.'"

I left the room before my anger spilled over its thin walls. Who knew anything? I stormed to myself. The crack through my composure had begun.

An intern saw me leave the office and came over. The struggle I was having must have been fully apparent. "Would you like to talk a minute?" she asked, and introduced herself. I said yes, I would, in a not-too-steady voice. We went to the cafeteria and had a cup of tea. "What is it you're most afraid of?" she asked, and I liked her soft manner and hard question.

"Tomorrow," I said. "His becoming a medical specimen."

"He's your son, isn't he? The son of your spirit?"

I couldn't answer, but I hoped something in me communicated how much I felt women like her had to bring to medicine. In the subsequent years, Carlos had so many generous and caring doctors, I put aside the one with the pipe.

I walked the corridors of the hospital when Carlos fell into a heavy sleep, and then I went outside and looked over the Salt Lake Valley. The hospital was up in the foothills, and the view was magnificent. Off to the west, Great Salt Lake gleamed in the sunlight. I thought of my Montana friend, Thelma Myzeld. Her last name had become a joke between us. She'd said "Myzeld" in class once, mispronouncing "missled." I don't even remember what her last name was. I wished I could have a chat with her, watch her linger over a cigarette. I'd like to have heard what she'd tell me. Then I did hear her—that whisky baritone. *God, Jeri, this is the true bad hand. These aren't good cards, Jeri, but you're holding them,* and I could see her tap the ash from her cigarette.

I turned to the mountain that literally loomed behind the hospital and walked up the twenty or thirty steps to the parking lot. I took the upper road that ended in brush and wildflowers. I followed it until I could take the little trail—almost everybody missed it—that led to Red Butte Canyon. Once in a while I'd turn and look out over the valley that extended twenty miles north and south. Houses sprawled all along the eastern foothills and all the way west to the shores of the Great Salt Lake. I wondered how this city and this wilderness could coexist so close together—the urban valley straight up against the forest.

I went higher and higher up into the foothills whenever I could take a break from Carlos's bedside. I found where the scrub oak gave way to a few pines and an occasional juniper. If I went far enough, I came to patches of shade and I could quit watching for rattlesnakes on the big rocks in the sun. Water streamed down beside the trail, sometimes running right into it so I had to wade for a few feet. It was still and quiet and it smelled like my cabin—nothing like the sterile smell of the hospital.

Carry his spirit with you, I said to myself. Bring something of him here to rest.

I found peace in the canyon, and comfort.

"Will you tell him he is going to die if he doesn't have a transplant or go on dialysis? You seem to be getting through to him better than anyone else," Carlos's doctor said to me the next morning on his rounds.

"How?" I'd looked up and asked, but he was already busy with his pipe, getting it ready to light as soon as he had an opportunity.

I fell into that discussion much sooner than I'd thought I would. In fact, just a few hours after I had talked with his doctor that morning, Carlos entreated me, without words, to tell him what was ahead.

"What will happen if you do nothing when you go home?" I asked, sitting on the bed beside him, our hands laced together in the way of children and for some reason I remembered Einstein saying, "I try to think like a child."

Carlos shrugged his shoulders and mouthed silently, "I don't know."

"You won't make it." He looked bewildered. "You will die," I added.

Three words. Make it as simple as you can, I was thinking.

"Do you know how fast?" Dear God, I thought, I'm saying this as though it were a dinner selection in order to say it at all.

Carlos shook his head. There was no alarm or fright in him, only a terrible attentiveness.

"In about one week," I replied. "Maybe three. The doctors say the longest you could live would be six months." I raised the fingers of one hand and the index finger of the other. He squinted his eyes and cocked his head in his attentive manner of questioning.

"Yes, little Fish, little Swimmer," I said, remembering his nicknames, "if you hadn't come to the hospital this time, you would be in big trouble now. Maybe you'd be gone." I could see he understood gone. *I don't know anything* was what his expression said. He didn't look that sick to me. He was still brown, and the weight loss didn't show yet in his finely made face. I felt encouraged.

We had the hundredth talk about kidneys "cleaning" the blood, about the poisons in his body with no way to get out. I made notes on a piece of paper as I went along so that he could look back and keep it all in mind.

"If you want to live," I said, "you have to take a chance." I had taught him the phrase *take a chance.* He used to chirp it out. It was right there with *up with everything.*

I wrote most of the rest as I talked. Carlos watched my hand, not my mouth.

YOU CHOOSE

I	II	III
Dialysis 2 times a week 2 hours a day or more	New Kidney Maybe from Robert The doctors would operate in about two months	If you do nothing, you will die

It might have been the worst moment I'd had in life until then—putting that piece of paper before him. He stared at the page. I could feel the words come up off its white surface and pass into him with their news. Images of Carlos were still running through my mind. I'd gotten good at that. I was seeing him dash through the graveyard, his beat-up gladiola held before him, his band of renegades coming after. "Che Guevara," I said to him. "Little Revolutionary." But I'd already forsaken the comparison; Carlos had none of Che's self-serving qualities if he did share a little of his passion for staging. This was the way I let go of the terrible moment—I diverted myself. I sat there thinking none of us would have paid attention to Che if we hadn't loved saying his name—the pure pleasure of saying *Che Guevara.* And then I was back to the moment. Carlos and I had never had the talks about the heroes of his heritage. "I wanted to take you to New Mexico to walk in the footsteps of Escalante," I said to him. He didn't look up, and so didn't "hear" any of it. Ten minutes must have gone by in silence while the words I'd written did their work. I ruffled his hair, helpless, trembling inside for him, for all of us.

He spoke finally, putting a finger on Column I. "All my life?"

"All your life," I answered.

"Every week?" he asked.

"Yeah, every week. If you stop, you will be sick again." I looked at him. "And yeah, it can make you die, Carlos." I tried to keep from saying, "My Carlos, my dear, dear Carlos."

We didn't talk about the kidney transplant, about the six weeks in the hospital, the risk, the lifelong subjugation to medical help. I said only, "If you have the operation, it will take a long time to recuperate—your body has to get used to it."

"Three," I said, as he stared at that column. "Some people want to die when a part of their body is worn out. What do you think?"

Again the shrug, almost imperceptible now. "I don't know," he said, so quietly I barely heard him. Then he said, "I'm afraid."

"I'm afraid too," I told him.

"Nothing's good."

TUBES, BLOOD TESTS, operations, preparations for more tests, interns asking the questions they had asked the day before—that became Carlos's life. Everyone was busy around him, but he had gone far away. I think he knew it all for what it was, life disconnected, a kind of macabre dance to keep from admitting that leaves do turn and fall. We all were becoming interlopers blundering through our concept of his body. Did we want to make him a fiberglass relic, anything in order to preserve him?

I did what Carlos couldn't do. I kept living in the world. I read about Vladimir Nabokov's death. It rained and I walked out in it and watched the tiny droplets hang from blades of bluegrass. I went up into the foothills. I'd worked out a series of trails, and I walked them every day, many miles through sage and wildflowers and golden grasses, ending in the pines of Red Butte Canyon. I brought Carlos bouquets of wildflowers—blue lupine and little purple fleabane and white-and-yellow mule's ears and red red Indian paintbrush and baneberry—probably baneberry, white and spherical. I would tell him the names as I placed them in a jar of water. I brought him a drawing pad and asked him to draw the flowers. "How?" he asked. Some days he wouldn't say much more than that.

"You know how better than I do," I told him. "That's about all I do anymore, and I learned it watching you." I took the charcoal pencil I'd brought and drew the great horned owl I'd seen on the trail. I did anything I could think of to divert the young man I still thought of as a boy, although he'd begun almost overnight to look old and wise.

I found myself going over and over in my mind the business of the body and what it learns to do, the indignities as well as the ecstasies it brings us. I'd heard Jonathan Miller talking on television a few months earlier about a strange psychological process. Some people evacuate themselves from some part of their body, he'd said—a hand, for example, which they want taken away with the breakfast tray. The strange dissociation was a last choice, I supposed, and I knew Carlos had left far more than a hand.

Jonathan Miller quoted the only funny thing I remember hearing about pain. An old woman in a Dickens novel, when asked if she was in pain, replied, "There is a pain somewhere in the room, but I can't be certain I've got it." British accent—*I cahn't be cehtain I've go-t it.* Remembering how I'd laughed helped.

Oddly enough, Jonathan Miller had ended talking about the blind and the deaf and our attitudes toward them. The blind make fools of themselves, he set forth, whereas the deaf make fools of us, asking us to repeat and repeat. Anything is ludicrous a third time. That, he claimed, is why we laugh at an ear trumpet but never at a white stick.

And so I was back to thinking about language and what it means to our lives. I had a thousand words for every one Carlos had, and, at this level, what more did I understand, really? Would his experience be profoundly different if he knew the words *capillary, fatty tissue, end renal disease*?

When Carlos had come out of the anesthesia after one of his surgeries, he had been signing. In the recovery room, watching his hands jump into life for a moment and twitch out a message, I wondered what we'd all been doing trying to tell deaf people how to communicate, how not to. Was signing, despite all our efforts to make him oral, the most natural mode of communication for Carlos? In how many ways do we impose our system of communication—or our preference within a system—upon each other?

At the ebb tide of his illness, Carlos quit talking altogether. Then one day he handed me a sheaf of drawings. I saw at a glance that they were unsigned. But I didn't ask him why. Before me was something that spoke far beyond the lines of the page. The die was cast for him and his amazing sketches record the realization, with loving consideration. What he caught in them for me is the mystery of a mind and the things that come together at the moment of flurry—in one a forest full of trees and a disappearing road; in another a skull and bones and a bird in the sky above a ponderous canyon. In a final one everything is out of joint—from the sign on the wrong side of the street to the sunset; the live tree on one side of the street, the dead one on the other; the blooming flower beside the one with its head bowed; birds, odd clouds, a tornado far down the road that comes to an abrupt end.

I had no need to ask why they all echoed the same plunge into the unknown, with its incredible unity of separation and peace. It was enough to have the record of what Carlos had conceived, consciously or unconsciously, in a kind of primeval expression, more accurate, far deeper than my profusion of words.

55

"Told you worry too soon."

I FOUND UNEXPECTED SOLACE in an exchange with a doctor who had all the qualities Carlos's first doctor lacked. She more than restored my confidence in the beautiful role a real professional can play in extraordinary circumstances. I met her while I was involved in a particularly interesting aspect of my work at that time as Director of Women's Programs at Westminster College. It was a liberal arts college, private and beautiful. Its campus was spread over twenty-seven acres of pines, cottonwoods, scrub oak, river birches. Mill Creek meandered between stately brick buildings decidedly Ivy League. The college was in Sugar House, which was even then a trendy part of Salt Lake City, a favorite of young people and not two miles from my own home. My position there was my first serious job since completing graduate degrees at the University of Utah and staying for several years to teach as an associate professor. I had initiated a lecture series at Westminster and in the wake of that, was asked to organize and participate in various city and state conferences. In one of those endeavors, I coordinated a conference for health care professionals. Dr. Rachel Remen was to give the keynote address, and several of us involved in the conference got acquainted with her the night before over dinner.

Dr. Remen, or Rachel, as she asked us to call her, was soft-spoken but she had a clean, tough mind and an irresistible delivery, even around a dinner table. She talked in a hushed voice, and the modulations were subtle. You found yourself leaning forward in order not to miss anything. On top of that, she said what you hadn't expected to hear.

Since the conference was focused on change in the medical world, she related a couple of experiences that had brought her to see how urgently change was needed. The first was an incident that defined an imbalance in the training doctors received at that time. It was a riveting story, told quietly—a combination I couldn't resist.

She had been a senior resident at Cornell. As the leader of ward rounds, she pushed the cart containing charts to the rooms of the patients being discussed. She'd been on heavy doses of steroids for the Crohn's disease that had been diagnosed when she was sixteen. A consequence was severe osteoporosis. Partway though the rounds, she heard a crack and felt a sharp pain in her left leg. Rather than tell the other residents, she got through the rest of the rounds by putting her weight on her right leg and leaning on the cart. She said she was dripping with sweat—she didn't mince words—by the time the rounds were over and the other residents left. It wasn't until then that she asked for help; she called a nurse over.

She returned to the ward the next day, her leg in a cast. Not one of the residents she'd been with asked about the cast or the fracture. "That's how much you didn't show weakness," she said, adding that weakness wasn't really what you'd be showing. She'd gone on to become Head of Pediatrics at Stanford Medical School and had recently left that assignment to help form and direct the Institute of Humanistic Medicine with a group of other doctors in San Francisco. She is known today for her books and for her work as medical director of the Commonweal Cancer Help Program.

Dr. Remen began her talk at the conference with an account of an experience she had had as an intern. She had been the only woman in the group of training doctors, and other interns would come to her door periodically, knock on it, and say to her, "My patient is crying. Can you come?" She told us that she would go with the intern, talk to his patient, try to find out what was happening, offer some comfort, then set about finding the intern who had usually wandered off to a lab. A subtle smile preceded, "There was never a word of thanks." She paused. There were nods. "I resented being summoned like this," she told us. "I considered it unprofessional." The soft voice, the real news.

"The reason I was called," she went on, "was that I was a woman. I was supposed to be good at this." And then she described herself at that time. "I was intellectual, I was individual, I was driven, I was judgmental. I had as many of the masculine principles as anyone in the shop."

Dr. Remen was tall and striking, her dark hair just beginning to show gray. She had a great calmness and composure. Unlike a lot of visiting lecturers, she wasn't offering herself as a visual aid. She presented herself straightforward, unadorned—talking about her own vulnerabilities in a way that made you see she used them as a route to understanding others, as the door to compassion. She wasn't hiding anything. I liked her immensely—we all did. I'm sure we each sat there having a personal revelation. I was thinking, *It can be done like this*—gracious and no nonsense and as honed as the edge of steel. She told us in that commanding but quiet voice of hers that she began to learn about a whole other world with those troubled patients she'd been summoned to help—a world where you allowed yourself to be responsive, a world made up of love, devotion, human strength, one that had a great deal to do with healing. "It became the secret world I shared with my patients," she said and noted that it was then that she began to add compassion and intuition to the technical skills she'd acquired. I remember exactly how she described the effect on her. "It made a great deal of difference in the way I saw myself," she told us.

I was listening as though my life depended on this doctor. Carlos's quality of life did depend on such a view, which was not often expressed in the seventies. She went on to talk about the need to balance what she called the masculine and feminine principles. She hoped to see these brought into a proper relation to each other as doctors promoted the quality of a patient's life while preserving physical health. "Along the way," she said, "we may discover the nature and purpose of our own lives. In that journey each medical professional should come to honor and respect that central, individual place within us which is our own—

not something learned, more like something remembered. We cannot simply call for change. We must *come* to this change." She ended with talking about the barriers—the fear of judgment as we seek our own way of learning who we really are. She drew the analogy between a doctor and a gardener. Gardeners use scientific knowledge, she told us, and something more.

At the end of the conference I thanked her from a place deep within me. I was surprised to hear myself mention Carlos. I couldn't say much; I was so moved I could barely keep a handle on what I was feeling. She reached into her purse, removed a card from her wallet, turned it over, and wrote her home phone number on the back of it. I watched as she extended to me the compassion she'd been talking about. She handed the card to me and took my arm. "If I can be of help, call me," she said. "It won't matter what time it is." I could feel such life in her, such profound attention to what I was struggling with. Her rich and elegant spirit flowed out of her like a current. I could still feel the infusion of strength and calm that Rachel had bestowed as I went back to Room 632. "Look like you stopped worrying," Carlos said to me when I came in. "Told you worry too soon." His words spoke worlds about how I'd been. I had brought apprehension with me into his sphere, not steadiness and assurance.

"Look good not to worry too soon, Jeri," he said, and I buried my face in the ragged cut-off brown shirt that barely covered his chest.

"Everybody crazy."

SOMETHING CHANGED FOR CARLOS too, and maybe part of it was my finding my way to a kind of calm. Carlos surprised everyone. The "enormous compliance" that was required was well within him. He was independent in assuming responsibility for getting to the hospital's dialysis unit and he was unerring in taking his eight or nine pills every day.

In the nine months that he remained on dialysis, I drove the distance between our two towns to visit him at least once a week, usually while he was being dialyzed.

Those scenes have always been hard for me to revisit, but they continue to extend my sense of Carlos. They added admiration to the mix. I got to see what he brought to the group of people who sat while the red tubes strung them toward a little more life. He did pantomimes, he called the technicians "vampires"—he made everybody laugh a dozen ways. Before he'd been there a month, half the floor was signing and teasing with him. He knew everyone, and not just how long they'd been sick or how often they came to the hospital. He knew whose son was in trouble, whose grandfather had just got home from California.

We rounded up an old Cougar XR-7 for him so that he could get to the hospital easily and have some tiny source of diversion as well. He watched television during the day or tinkered with his car and played with Linda's baby, whom he adored. He was always the one to bathe him, and he was so protective of the little fellow, I had to laugh. "No one chased you around like that, terrified you'd have dirty hands, Carlos," I'd kid him.

"Meybe he be sick," he answered. That had become his deepest fear, and not just for himself, I could see. Everything that could contaminate the boy had to be put out of reach. The garbage itself had to be kept miles from where he played. Carlos and his boy were wonderful to see together—their understanding of each other expressed not in words so much as in a felt language.

Linda had been fascinated by Carlos and his unusual combinations of language, and even more by his hands, sending words silently through the space between him and his friends. She loved to see him sign. I understood that; it was like watching a poem being shaped in the air. I also thought of our primate ancestors and their dexterity in trees. Carlos's hands owed a debt to them. But Linda became sulky and withdrawn toward the end of Carlos's first month of dialysis. I didn't think of myself as her mother-in-law, but I did ask myself to go the extra mile for the woman Carlos had chosen. Her life was restricted not simply by Carlos's deafness but now by his illness. I wondered what would become of their marriage now that he needed help.

When one of the technicians called me at the end of March and told me Carlos had requested, "Get Jeri, she's fast," I laughed. But I wasn't laughing when I got to the hospital and saw his face.

"What's the matter?" I asked.

"Wait," he said, and not until we'd left the dialysis wing of the hospital and were seated across from each other in a restaurant would he speak. "I will tell *you,* that's all," he began, and recounted his story. He had come home, put his key in the door, stepped inside, and found his furniture, his wife, the baby he had taken for his own, gone. He stood looking at an empty apartment. Now, turning to me with agony in his eyes, he asked, "Why?"

"Oh my dear," was all I could say. I was having a very bad time with anger and trying not to express it.

After a while he asked, "Is it my car? Linda says you want it to be hers."

That did it for me. "I'll get your car for you tonight," I said to him. "Where is Linda now?" He told me she was at her parents', and that they had been rough with his brother Robert when he'd tried to get the car. Robert was no slouch, but his failure to get that car did not dissuade me. "Don't worry, I'll get it," I said. Carlos had never seen me so resolved, and it amused him enough that I could see him forget his heartache for a moment and warm to the hunt. Even in this circumstance, the way we loved an adventure together rose to the surface. Bonnie and Clyde came to mind but that was about the worst comparison I could have made.

We went together to the house. The car was there, blocked by three other cars. I went in, was turned away, *really* turned away, bullied. I made a second effort, this time not allowing myself to be pushed aside. Carlos was waiting outside, and I was glad I hadn't let him be witness to belligerence. I walked past the protesting mother, the caught-off-guard father—naked to his shorts. Linda sat in the kitchen having a permanent. That smell soaked through everything. It was as though it issued up from the torn stuffing on the dining room chairs, the sacks of garbage, the jumble of knickknacks, the crosses, the dirty dishes. It was a disheartening scene and I could see that Carlos having insisted on perfectly clean space for his boy might have originated here. "Get me the keys," I said to Linda.

A woman feels pretty subdued with her wet hair in little twisting curlers and permanent wave fluid drifting down her forehead, but it didn't take the stubbornness out of Linda. "I don't have the keys—ask my father," she said. Her words flashed up at me. And then my own anger took over. I took a step toward her with each word I spoke.

"You have them. You get them. I'm perfectly happy to call the police and have them get the keys, but you'd be smart, Linda, to get them." I was standing right over her by the time I said *You'd be smart to get them.* She got up, walked over to a counter and picked them up, and came over and slammed them down on the table.

I felt the fingers of fear at the back of my neck as I moved quickly past her brother and her father. Carlos saw me come out in a hurry and he came to my side. "You drive my car," I said, handing him the keys. I drove his car across the lawn and down a sidewalk to maneuver out of the blockade set up around it.

"Why so fast?" Carlos asked, as nervous as I was, when we got to his apartment. I sank in a chair and realized what a chance I'd taken getting both our throats slit in the part of town where a demand was an invitation to a knife.

"You're fast," Carlos exclaimed, and I said, "Damn right." Then I added, "I'm crazy," and went home, wondering how Carlos could manage living alone.

"Linda and baby like ghosts for me," he told me one night. "They stay in the house for me." *Family* had been his favorite word for the years he'd been with Linda and her boy, and he was plainly lost without them.

In an effort to distract him, I threw down a map a few weeks before Easter and said, "Let's take a trip."

"Can't leave," he said.

"You can for two or three days. And if you need to be dialyzed, I'll get you to a hospital." I could see that the idea filled him with terror, but I wanted him not to conceive of himself as a prisoner of his medical regimen, so I persisted. I kept suggesting we fly to San Francisco or Las Vegas, and I'd spin yarns about those towns while he sat in the dialysis unit. I spread a map out on his table and said, "You pick." I showed him where New York was and Boston, and above it, Montreal.

I thought he'd forgotten all about my attempt to spring him when he drove up in front of my house the day before Easter, decked out in new Levi's and a vest, and said, "Las Vegas." We whirled into our old rapture at an excursion, making plans to leave the next day.

He went home for the night. I watched him drive away and sat up late reading about Las Vegas, that outpost turned fantasy. I got up early the next morning, wondering if Carlos would grow afraid of leaving the familiar technicians who knew how to keep the delicate balance. I had time to feel some fear myself. Then suddenly he was there, a brilliant new maroon shirt under his embroidered vest.

We chatted on the plane, we counted our money, watched over a silver wing for Las Vegas to spread itself across the desert. It appeared the mirage that it is, an improbable greenbelt cut through the tumbleweed.

By the time we landed, I could see that nothing would have amused Carlos more than this highly visual, glittering island of escape. He'd never seen a palm tree, or a taxi driver as wild as ours was. And the hotel was pure astonishment to him, with its giant waterwheel and its lobby full of slot machines and gaming tables and throbbing crowds—from the very wealthy to the truly strange. He hadn't watched five minutes before he looked at me and announced, "Same you. Everybody crazy!"

We roamed the town for the afternoon, riding the bus along the strip—now garish, now elegant—and downtown to Fremont Street. Then we went back to our hotel, dressed—I mean really dressed—and sallied into the casino to try our luck. I played craps and Carlos strolled through the rows of slot machines. I lost track of him for a while, and when I found him, he was sitting at a blackjack table placing five-dollar bets. Everyone at the table was protective of him—and clearly intrigued. Even in this no-holds-barred setting, he stood out. I watched him for a while as he sat there at the table with his small hands holding his cards, scratching for a hit as deftly as the little squirrel-boy who so many worlds ago had imitated a wave coming in. Even the dealer, it was apparent, hoped to see him prevail. For some reason I thought of Melville's *The Confidence-Man*, and I took it all in, this little lad making his way in such a double-edged world.

We walked to the Flamingo and saw the dinner show. Carlos had wanted to see "the girls with nothing," and he loved it. He called over a roving photographer, flashed her a twenty-dollar bill, and had our picture taken. Where had he learned to do these things? Sick as he was and worried as I was, we both look very young in that photograph—and happy. Then we tasted champagne and gambled at every casino on the way back to our hotel.

I didn't last as long as Carlos. By midnight I said to him, "Don't go too far. There's a lot to do right here in the hotel. Think I'll sneak up to our rooms."

"Won't far," he said. "Won't long." And he corrected himself. "Won't *be* too long."

When the phone rang, I'd been asleep for what seemed like hours. I woke with that kind of start that brings every night fear into focus with the switching on of an unfamiliar light. Carlos wasn't in his room, I could see that from where I was as I picked up the phone. I filled with dread. Maybe I shouldn't have left him down there alone—that was my first thought.

It was a long-distance person-to-person call to me. A clearly irritated voice began. "Carlos Salazar is scheduled for a kidney transplant in a few hours. He must be in Salt Lake City as quickly as possible. The longer he waits, the less chance the kidney has of being accepted."

I was dumbfounded. "Who is this?" I asked. "Does Carlos know he is scheduled for a transplant? Has he agreed to that?"

It was a medical counselor, one who was damned mad at me for having him out of town. "Wait a minute," I finally said. "Everyone at the hospital has my number. Everyone knew he was leaving, including his dialysis unit. If Carlos was not to be taken out of town, I should have known that. And certainly he should have. And his family. Now start again."

She calmed down. "Can you get him here?"

I wondered about a private flight, but I knew small planes didn't make it to Salt Lake City in a few hours, and it would take that much time to arrange.

"I don't see how," I replied. "It's 2:00 a.m. There isn't a flight out of here until morning."

"I don't know when he'll get another chance," she said. "I don't know *if* he will."

She hung up and I stared at the ceiling, wondering whether I could find Carlos in the nightlife of Las Vegas if I got up and got dressed. And if I *could* find a private plane. And what would I tell him?

When he walked into the room, he was as animated as he'd been when I first saw him. "I won!" he exclaimed. "People like me!" He threw down handfuls of silver dollars and a tiny porcelain dog. "For you," he said. "For thank you."

We talked for a while, and finally I told him about the phone call. He went to the window and looked down at the shimmering town. When he turned around, he said, "Will home in the morning," which changed our plans by a day.

"It will be too late for the transplant," I told him. He looked both sick at heart and relieved. I hadn't realized it, but that covered it for me too. I could often look at Carlos's face and discover more clearly my own feelings.

Across the room from me, he snapped his fingers in his mock *tough luck* gesture and said, "It's okay."

But the fun had gone out of the trip, and we packed quietly the next morning and took a van to the airport. We were silent on the flight home, each sorting out what a kidney transplant would mean. As soon as we landed in Salt Lake City, I drove Carlos to his mother's house in Ogden. On the way he said, "Why you do thees for me? Take me Las Vegas? Take me Montreal with you?"

"To keep you off the streets," I said. It wasn't at all funny. I'd never had perfect timing. But I let time go by now. I was quiet for a few miles. Then I tried again. "I do this because I want to and because I can. A lot of love is in there somewhere. And you pay back big dividends—two to one—like those games back there."

His family all came out to meet us. At the car window, he leaned to say what sounded like "goodbye, my love." Lilly looked at me, tears just behind her smile as she repeated mysteriously what he had said, knowing, as I did, how he had meant *love.*

"I care, dead or alive."

ANOTHER CALL DID COME summoning Carlos to the hospital for a kidney transplant. It was 1978—I don't remember what season. I remember how Carlos looked by then; he could have been seventy-eight. He was thin yet swollen from taking prednisone, bent, going gray, losing his hair. He wore a beard but the swelling in his face was still visible. He was twenty-five, a year older than I had been when I met him. I was thirty-nine.

I speed up in my mind what happened after that call. Everything moved with alarming swiftness anyway. Since it was in Salt Lake City and quite near my place, I was the first to arrive at the hospital. I waited for an hour, counting the minutes, which were crucial. The image of Carlos fleeing into the foothills and away from his fate came back to me. And I had one of those crazy thoughts only time and history can give you. I'd like to be back there. That was manageable.

Another half hour went by, and still Carlos didn't walk into the hospital lobby. I phoned Lilly. "He said he'd be back," she told me, worry spreading between us. For myself, I didn't know if I wanted him to be on time for what was ahead. Two hours went by. I remembered having seen a kidney kept alive in a machine. It had looked, from where I stood, like a heart.

When Carlos walked into the hospital, Linda was with him, and I understood that he had gone and found her before he was rushed through admissions, preparations, blood tests, compatibility tests, the signing of a document that listed endless risks, including a sentence about the possibility of losing life.

Then suddenly he was being strapped to a gurney, wheeled quickly toward the waiting kidney. I walked beside him to the big double doors. Linda was there, unsure, afraid. Lilly and Robert had left. I think Lilly really couldn't bear to see her son wheeled into surgery. He looked at us as long as he could see us from his swiftly moving table.

When he was just outside the operating room, the attendant stopped for a minute so we could catch up and tell him goodbye. He reached no-longer-firm arms around me and whispered, "Pray for me." I was memorizing him. Then he added the sentence that taught me more about how to live life than anything he'd said, or done. He'd pulled me down to him so his face was against my ear and I couldn't see him. But I heard, "I care, dead or alive."

I watched him embrace Linda, whisper something, and then he was moving again. His face was the last thing we saw as he turned on the gurney to look at us for a moment longer. There were the dark eyes, more heavily lashed than when he was a boy. Even with his beard, he still looked more boy than man, but the eyes said something different.

The doors closed behind him, and I stood there fumbling with Thomas's phrase, "Lord, I believe. Help thou mine unbelief." I went to my copse, my stand of trees in Red Butte Canyon, and wished again that Thelma Myzeld were around. I pressed against the warm earth and prayed for Carlos.

As I watched him in the recovery room six hours later, I thought how trapped, how absolutely fixed he was by that beautiful, failing body of his. He could not say, "I am leaving you," and be done with it—not so far as we know life, or at least not so easily.

Blank days followed. There was considerable pain, a second, and eventually a third and fourth surgery, and then it seemed like endless surgeries. Then infection, and through it all the wait to see if the kidney would be rejected.

Carlos was overwhelmed by the extensiveness of the medical attention, and the interminable length of every day. One incident can stand for the thousands of them—all confounding, disorienting. Each chunk of ice he was allowed was accounted for. He was not permitted a drink for many days, and he was almost crazy with thirst and with wondering why he couldn't drink. The medications he was taking further confounded him. When he was finally allowed a glass of water, he looked at me as though I'd tricked him and asked, "Why did you bring milk?" Every perception seemed to have been altered. If I brought him ice, he asked me to take it back and get ice. I'd sit by his bed and say, "Carlos, look, this *is* ice," and he'd say, "Maybe *look* like ice, but it's hot." As the complexities and confusions unfolded, my explanations were more and more inadequate.

It was a long road to the extraordinary adjustment Carlos eventually made to his situation. What has endured for me are those moments, framing a capacious soul. One of them was his response to betrayal. What was left of the life he had known with his wife and son, which had been on-again, off-again after she'd left the apartment, dissolved while he was away from them. He met the raw news that Linda was to have another baby, again not his, with a cry that sent nurses scurrying to his room. But they learned nothing about any dimension of his physical health. By the time they got to him, he had already turned to the wall.

That evening he wrote me a note with instructions that I was not to open it until I had left his room. He hugged me goodnight earlier than usual, but it was a different embrace from his customary nuzzling, animal fondness. This was an embrace beached, run up on a sandbar.

I read his note on the way to the elevators. "I have a big problem," it said. "Nowhere home."

Almost at once he put that part of his life aside—at least as far as any of us could see. When his wife came again, he told her, "I will not be your fool." Even now I can't imagine how he got there so quickly, so definitively. And how he put together such a sentence—part philosophy, part idiom.

My first concern was where he would live when he was released from the hospital. "Nowhere home" was only part of what faced him. He would need not only a place to go but someone to help. That problem he seemed to know he could not solve while he was in the hospital, and he said to me over and over, "Will be okay. Wait and see."

Lilly came to find me in the hospital cafeteria one night when we had both come to visit Carlos. She was worried that I hadn't stayed when she came into his room. I'd wanted them to have time alone. "I don't get much chance to visit with you," she said when she found me. "I like you to stay with us." Walking beside her on the way back down the hall to his room, I felt how entirely she had accepted me as part of the family. Her caring for him had lifted her beyond any contest on a field of jealousy that might have been.

Just before we got to Room 632, she said in her wonderful accent, "I told Miranda I don't know what I would have done all these days if you hadn't been here in Salt Lake to help Carlos. I couldn't have gotten along without you." Lilly was anything but effusive, and so I valued her words all the more.

She talked to me that night of her young womanhood, of her husband Aurelio and how he was killed, of Carlos as an infant. She ended telling me she had been to see the son she'd given away while he was a baby. She hadn't seen him for eighteen years, and, as she talked, I hoped he had learned what kind of woman she was when he met his mother—a woman who had had the courage to find him after so long and who had had the selflessness to let him go to someone who could provide the many surgeries his severe medical problems required.

Here was a woman who had had to give up one child, who had lost her husband when she was still young, who had shared Carlos and who would lose him and Ernie as well, who would see Edwin go to the state penitentiary for a good part of his life, and who would lose her cherished, beautiful daughter Miranda to what Carlos thought was suicide. Through all of it, she had held the shrinking band of her family together.

What do I, or most of us, know of loss?

"What happened, that's all."

CARLOS CONTINUED TO HAVE periods of retreat from the world, but gradually we began to talk as we never had. In those hours, waiting to see what would happen, he went over and over the details of his life, discovering for himself as well as for me what it had meant to him.

I asked him once during our conversations what the first thing he remembered was. "I don't know," he answered, surprised and almost confused by the question, or more likely, by the reason for my asking it. Later, in response to my repeated quizzing, he tapped his head in his grandly feigned manner of annoyance and said, "I told you. Straw for brains." Whatever the variations of his answer, he'd always end shrugging his shoulders and saying, "Nothing. Remember nothing."

I approached the question with what I thought were brilliant devices to stir memories in him that he had forgotten and I wanted to keep alive. Had he lived on Patterson Avenue as a baby? Did he remember when his father died? What was his first room like? Who was his first friend? What was his first day of school like? But nothing would jar the memories of his early life—not details from mine, nor my string of questions. Since he had never talked about or been reminded of those days, they had faded and been lost.

Then one afternoon he looked up at me and exclaimed, "King Kong!" I couldn't understand him and we weren't talking about the first thing he remembered so I hadn't a notion what he was saying or what it related to. To make matters worse, *k's* were among his least intelligible sounds, coming out with an effortful burst that placed them close to guttural *g's* and sometimes *d's*. At last he spelled the words, his deft hands moving swiftly, beautifully to form the letters. Still I struggled. "One more time," I asked him.

After Carlos had exhausted almost all his wits, and certainly his patience, I cried out in triumph, "King Kong!" He was not as enthusiastic.

"Slow!" he exclaimed, loving for a minute to be the one who knew instead of the one struggling to know. I was indeed hopelessly slow whenever he fingerspelled or signed. I did a little better with signing, but I recognized only a handful of the thousand gestures Carlos knew for words and whole concepts.

I was still pronouncing "King Kong," heartened that I'd finally been able to hold all the letters in my mind long enough to read them. Carlos shook his head, determined not to admire me as much as I was admiring myself. He ended up laughing at his poor student and went on to tell me that when he was a little boy, he woke up scared after seeing *King Kong* on television, and he went into his mother's room and slept with her.

"First thing I remember," he said.

I was ecstatic at Carlos having come upon an early memory. I recalled my own response to that compelling bit of lore, and I asked, "Were you sad when King Kong died?"

He didn't understand the question. I repeated it, using my hands to remind him of the scene in which King Kong's mighty and gallant heart pumps its last. But that was not what he didn't understand, which I realized when I tried another tack.

"Were you sad for him? He was alone."

"No," Carlos replied. He rarely revised his initial response to something, whatever position someone else held. "What happened, that's all."

I became doubly intrigued with Carlos's history and the identity encased in it after that. Especially early in his life, it had taken virtually everything he had to deal with the daily demands of "Are you hungry?" "Where is your coat?" "What do you want?" The difficulty of making his way in a hearing world left no room for the acquisition at the same time of any sense of his own history. Few deaf people unfold in the richness of listening to a mother and father, friends and teachers, retelling, keeping alive, the endearing stories that set them apart from other children. "You used to crawl along licking the rug when you were little." "You loved dust." "You flew before you could walk—flew in an ecstasy off any piece of furniture when your Daddy came home from work." This exterior view of self that for most of us accumulates into a sense of personal history had never been given to Carlos.

He didn't remember the day he realized he was deaf, if there was a day rather than a slowly gathering understanding. Once, in Montreal, he had asked me quite matter-of-factly if he would be able to hear when he died. Not long before he did die, he said to me about his deafness, "It's okay. I don't care."

I took that occasion to ask him if he knew he was smart. "No," he answered, and then his expression turned playful. "I want to be the same," he said.

"You're not the same," I kidded him. "You're not the same in brains and you're not the same in looks." After awhile I went on, "You know you're handsome. You like that, don't you?"

"Yes, I'm happy with thees," he answered, making a circle around his face with his hand. It was the sign for beauty.

I persisted, although I knew he would not be serious again. Would he change anything—in his looks, his life?

"No," he assured me. He had only wanted to change one thing and that he had done. Swiftly as a frog's tongue, he ran a finger down the part in the center of his hair. "Een the middle, not the side," he concluded about his looks, and no doubt his life as well, laughing at how he'd managed to deflate the question.

Enticed by Carlos's first memory, I asked Lilly about his early days. Her bits of information led me to remember 1953, the year he was born. I had been a freshman in high school.

As a baby, Lilly told me, Carlos was tiny and he didn't say much. In fact, he didn't say anything, although he made sounds.

When she took him to school at age five, a doctor told her that something was wrong with her son, and she went home with him, silent and heartsick. "Before long they found out about his hearing. He was a little bit the pet. My husband Aurelio always said I paid more attention to Carlos than to my baby Michael," she told me. "He was the one I had to give up."

Maybe she had more reason than she knew to be heartsick. Her Carlos represented a skew in any graph that sought to explain the unexamined norms of the time.

As though on some odyssey only I, of the two of us, could make, I began to gather information about the world Carlos was born into. I sat in the library and looked through copies of *Life* magazine from 1953. Men wore hats in ads. Their hair was well groomed with Vaseline Hair Tonic. The rich among them drove Cadillacs wherever they went, whatever they did. Coke in a bottle was a Natural, but only the young and the white were shown drinking or driving or grooming. Women tried to look like the model Suzy Parker, who went around saying, "I come from an average Ku Klux Klan family."

In the spotlights that Lilly barely had time to be aware of, Johnnie Ray was wailing "Cry," which became one of the top tunes of the year.

No more than a handful of women were alive to Eleanor Roosevelt's urgings for them to get in the game and stay in it. And no one took seriously Marilyn Monroe or the comment she made that extends, peculiarly, to every isolated group: "When you're famous you kind of run into human nature in a raw kind of way. People . . . say anything to you . . . and it won't hurt your feelings—like it's happening to your clothing."

The word *Chicano* had not yet become the controversial label of a people. Nor had Spanish-American, Mexican-American, or Hispanic replaced other epithets of the day. No one had yet applied *macho* to a style of behavior. Favor had continued to shift in the centuries since Spain was heralded for its famous trail, its colonizing. And Mexico was still declining in North American opinion. The role of the Mexican in the news was representative—the media continued to provide tales of an occasional local stabbing and to offer sidebars on "the war with the wetbacks."

What I was finding about 1953 cast a sad perspective, not so much on Carlos's life as on the era that claimed him. I thought again of other claims—the lost one to the land of the Pueblo and Colorado. Carlos Louis Salazar—named for his grandfather's brothers who were Spanish on the father's side, Irish on the mother's. A once-royal family had had a hard time stepping beyond prejudice as well as poverty in the early and middle decades of the twentieth century.

I ended up in Mexico and then New Mexico, gathering sand, stones, leaves to bring back to Carlos—but how to bring him the red hills at sunset, the rabbit brush, the legends he had never heard? What had become of the birthright of cedar and gold hidden in the arroyos his fathers had ridden?

On one of the graves outside Taos was written, "Memtoria, Memtoria." I took that phrase home with me, thinking again of the year 1953.

The recent world war that had dominated lives and imaginations as no other war had left the nation eager to celebrate what was usually thought of as the innocence of the times. The new peace was almost careless, ignoring as best it could the cries of the coming era that were already rising in the throat of the present one. Nearly everyone agreed with the Pennsylvania housewife who said, when Dwight D. Eisenhower was elected president, "It's as if America has finally come home."

Helen Keller's fingers had just "seen" the smile of that president—Helen, who spoke the way Carlos Salazar spoke. But Carlos did not remember having known the story of Helen Keller.

Even so, his life would become almost an index to the concerns of the next decade—the handicapped, the disadvantaged, the minority, the dropout, the drug enchanted, the refugee from marriage, the welfare case, the medical experiment.

Yet he seemed to be forgotten, or rather never known, by his own decade. He did not grow up seeing pictures of Suzy Parker in *Life* magazine, although he inherited some of the terror behind her glib comment. There was no Cadillac—and sometimes no car—in the driveway to take him wherever he went, whatever he did. He never used Vaseline

Hair Tonic, and Coke was not the Natural for him. His mother Lilly didn't see *The Robe* in 1953, although she prayed the morning she gave birth to Carlos.

What was to follow in her son's life was in many ways the story of a nation changing. If he "was trouble in school" and later, his was a trouble that was as universal as prejudice and as costly as indifference.

Little wonder he learned early on to observe, "What happened, that's all."

"I'm a jailbird."

THE FORTY DAYS Carlos was in the hospital following his kidney transplant seemed to come apart for him and make of themselves more days within the one endless Monday, the subsequent and even longer Tuesday, the raw, unspendable Wednesday. By Thursday he was beside himself with how to endure to the end of another week.

Talk was not enough, nor was television, nor every kind of invention with the few things he would or could eat. Nor did poker hold his attention. He began to read more than he ever had, but that was always discouraging business for him. What he needed was work.

I tried to imagine what I'd do if I were confined to one bed in one room with one hallway beyond to be explored in my few strong moments. Then I'd lose the thread of that pursuit and be back to searching for what Carlos could do that would claim his attention, really take him, and perhaps earn him some money. Nothing came to mind, and I'd jump back to wondering what I'd do if I were lying in that bed.

One day I saw a handsome portfolio in an office supply store. It was a portable writer's notebook with what appeared to be a leather exterior. Five minutes later I had it in Carlos's room, along with a box of pencils.

"You have a job," I exclaimed.

He laughed. "Can't work. Too ladzy."

"Laz-z-y," I said. "Yes, too lazy, but those days are over. Your car is a mess. How are you going to fix it when you get out of here? You need some money."

"Can't work," he insisted, enjoying being unavailable. "Too weaky."

"Listen, Weaky," I said, "you're working. You're a bum in here. Look at you—sleep all day, stroll around the ward in that ragged shirt. It's a shame."

He loved it, especially if he thought he'd been a spectacle. "I'm a jailbird," he returned. "I can't fly out."

At that I laughed. It was wonderful beyond measure to be back to laughing with Carlos, especially when jail had once been no laughing matter. "The job will fly to you, jailbird. If you don't snap at it, you'll be so poor when they spring you, you'll have to thieve a new battery and then you'll be jail *bait*." I signed a bit so he'd keep up with me.

"What job?" he asked finally, overtaken by the curiosity I'd counted on.

"Writer. Writer Carlos Louis—alias Fish—Salazar."

"I hate thees!" he exclaimed. "Miss Bentley made me write. What's that? A-lees?'"

"A-lee-es, alias," I repeated, taking his wrist as I'd done when he was a boy and tapping out the rhythm of the word. "It means 'another name.' Your other name is Fish, isn't it?"

"Ho!" came the sound of amused remembering. "I forgot."

"I did too and then the other day I remembered it."

Overnight he became marvelous company again. He hadn't been so engaged in months, and it made him all the more engaging.

"You were the best writer Marian ever had," I told him.

"Says who?" he threw back.

He always undid me when he came up with a familiar expression I had no idea he knew, making it somehow fresh.

"Says me," I answered. "People who understand writing can't be messed with. Somebody wants to lay a hundred dollars a page on you. Would prefer ten dollars a page but will go as high as a hundred."

"Same as pay?" he asked.

"Same," I said. "*Is* pay."

He calculated. I didn't want him to ask any more questions, but knew I'd just begun my campaign. The big one was next.

"What for?"

"Take my advice," I answered. "No questions—just take the big money and run."

I could see him thinking it over.

"About what?" he asked. You could practically see his thought process on his face.

"Write about what?"

"Yes. Nothing say."

"Wow, *good* language," I said. "'Nothing say!' One dollar a page for that."

"What I'm say?" he tried again. "Nothing *to* say. I told you, straw for brains."

We talked with real purpose now. Would he write about King Kong?

"No, finish!" he said, his voice going high on *finish*. His eyes were dancing, alive to the contest.

I didn't want to lose my fish. "Ten dollars a page," I said, tossing the pencils at him. "And no giant letters. A normal page—full." I left, wanting the offer to brew in that dazzling head of his. What were the stories he'd tell now—all these years since the fanciful notes, the touching letters, and the wild tales written at school? I realized as I took the elevator down I would really have paid a hundred dollars a page to find out.

When I came back the next morning, he scowled at me.

"Nothing sleep!" he threw down for openers.

"Ha!" I slapped my thigh. "See! I knew you were a writer. No writer can sleep! How much did you make? Ten bucks? Twenty bucks? Forty bucks?"

He got out his leather notebook and opened it surreptitiously. I tried to steal a glance, but he tucked it away from me. He leafed through pages. When he didn't stop, I thought he was kidding. But I'd gotten around to where I could see pages and pages full of his familiar handwriting. I was ecstatic.

"One hundred bucks," he said, looking up. "Maybe not enough."

"You mean you want a thousand? You wrote ten pages the first night? You'll break the bloody bank and be out of a job!"

"No. One hundred. Ten pages, yes. Ten dollars a page. One hundred—that's too much. Eet make me too quiet." He grinned at me. He was pleased with himself.

"So big money makes you quiet?" I asked. I couldn't wait to get my hands on what he had written. "Lemme see," I implored, reaching for the pages.

"Bad speech," he mocked.

I laughed, but mouthed for myself *lemme see* and *let me see.* "You can tell a difference?"

"Yes. Your tongue is different. Watch me," and he said the two phrases.

"You're so damn smart," I said, but he couldn't tell what I was saying because I was hugging him.

Even knowing he was brilliant and then some, I wasn't prepared for the private revelations and honest searchings of "Cathy's Story." I was thunderstruck. The carefully built skills in language had deteriorated, but what had survived was Carlos, pure and unfettered—vivid, highly selective, utterly honest. I thought of William Saroyan, who might have been speaking of him and Cathy in writing, "We are little children. Being frightened, we frighten each other. Try to understand. Try to love each other."

Cathy's Story

The first time I saw Cathy R. she walk by herself. I said Hi! Then another day she still walk alone. Both are shy. First time I talk to her, but she not understand. I leave her for a few day. Cathy talk to Manuel G. He told me she want to come over her house. I told Manuel how can I plan and what time? He told me, "I think it is funny." She wait for her mother and father to go some place. I watch her house when the lights on and off. That means come. But both still shy. She ask me she want to learn sign language.

Next day I ride the bicycle around block. She follow me. Both are hide from people. She ask me don't be afraid her parents. I said ok and try. Both ride and play. The sunny was go down and her mother look and look around the block. Cathy and I hide from her mother. She ran to home after awhile, then I was scared to go over to her house. Why Cathy told parents to know me and Cathy because she told them and talk about me. Cathy and I watched T.V. few hour. Her parents ask me, "Will you come and have dinner other day?" Her family and I went downtown for dinner. They pay for me. I think they were little nice to me.

Next day she have to baby-sit. Her mother name is Mary. Mary told me I can come over to her house anytime when Cathy worked baby-sit. Mary told me be careful and no outside. I said ok. Mary and Mike leave the house. We are alone. We final made love and kiss, but still shy because we are first time fall love.

When school was close for summertime, her family and I went to camp. Next fall I bought promise ring for her. She was happy. She ask me when I can get married. I said, "I want to finish my school." She told me can't wait. I was surprised. I ask her, "Why you can't wait?" She told me she hate her parents because they tell her to do work and work clean the house and baby-sit. She was tired of it. She was run away from home. Next day Mary came to my house and ask me have you seen Cathy R? I said no, I have not seen her. Mary was real mad and leave. Few hour Manuel came to my house. He told me, "I have met Cathy in store. She ask me where she can sleep and hide from her parents."

Cathy and I run away from home. We live with friend for two week. I saw my mother and Cathy's mother come. How they know where we was? They check his room and ask him, "Ever you seen Cathy and Carlos?" Bob told them no, but he lie to them.

Cathy still ask me when we can married. I told her wait. She ask me why? Because we are young, I told her. Cathy was 16 year old, I am 17 year old. She ask, "So what?" We was fight and mad and arguing. Next day I went back home.

She won't home. I leave and let her alone.

Few day Mary caught her downtown. Mary told my mother Carlos can't visit her house for two month. I was go out with other girl. I saw Gloria. She know I have girlfriend Cathy, but other girl not know. Gloria leave me alone. Gloria told Cathy about me. I was real mad. Gloria is a big mouth. She call cop. I don't run from cop. I wait for cop. I am Risk. Cop take me to jail for shove her. I have to jail for one week.

When I was out of jail, I went home. Manuel came to my house. He give me note from her. I read it. She said I am sorry, miss you. I love you. I think about it, ok. Could I go back girlfriend? Then we plan marry June 3, 1973.

My mother and I went over to Cathy's house. We talk and meet. Mary told me I have to drop out of school. But my mother told me, "It is up to you." Lilly is care of me. Because Cathy have a baby, that's why. But I still worried because I don't have car, job, other else. I said ok, well I will marry her in summertime. Baby was out of pregnant in March 13, 1973. But I still under school. Mary was baby sit for Cathy. Both still mad, fight, arguing.

Mary and Cathy went to see lawyer man. He sent me a letter. He want talk to me. I talk to him. I told him I want first finish my school. He said ok. Next day, I still worried because I don't want married her. She hit me. So I hit back. My family and Cathy's family fight and fight. Her brother try kill me, because he bring gun. But he never do it. Last time I see Charlie was two half month old. But now he was five years old.

A note was added at the bottom of "Cathy's Story," which, as far as I knew, was the first account Carlos had written of his life. It said:

"Jeri: I think it is not finish because it is little mistake.

You read it, change, I will write more.
ok

But there was no tampering with the strangely poetic, if unsettling, record of a life lived by imagination and I suppose imitation. I was troubled to see how Carlos had handled his frustration in protecting his independence and dumbfounded that he had been so insistent on finishing school. And I was astonished that he would let me see the inner seams of his life. I had a great respect for his honesty, and for his initiative.

"Maybe I will be work go go go boy."

AFTER THAT, CARLOS STOPPED the periodic turning away from the world. The staring at the wall and the terrible vacancy were gone from him for good. In its place were qualities I watched unfold with real regard.

I had told him at some point, "Ask people questions. It will help." Now when I walked through his doorway, he was full of inquiries about my life. "Did you play tennis today? Did you win?" "What happening at the office?" "Have you had lunch?" It was as though overnight he had learned how to move all his world outside himself.

Liveness came from everywhere within him. We were rarely alone after the beginning of those days. He was the fountainhead of entertainment for nurses, doctors, interns, patients, and of course for me. The medical staff all but neglected their duties to linger in his room and tease or be teased by him as he held court.

For the nurses who liked life a little spicy, he told jokes that made them blush. I didn't know he knew this variety—he would never repeat them to me. For the nurses who were intrigued with his deafness, he taught sign language. For the ones who were nervous in trying to communicate with him, he wrote notes.

"What you gonna do when you get out of here?" one of the nurses asked him almost daily. She was an unstoppable, redheaded, tough-talking woman, seemingly all crust, but no one was fooled. She spent half her time teaching Carlos to make a hook rug and then finished it for him.

"What's gonna happen to ya, ya little shit?" she asked again one night when I was there. She popped her gum and ruffled his hair. "What will you do when you don't have us to fool around with all day?"

"Meybe I will be work go go go boy," he told her. She loved it and was back in his room ten minutes later asking the go-go boy where he planned to work.

"No, meybe marry rich one," he laughed. "How much you have?"

Off she went again, slapping her thighs and mumbling, "Cutest damn little shit."

There was another nurse, Marilyn, and she took as good care of me as she did of Carlos. I could call her from home and get a report any time of the day or night. Another nurse, Cill, created good will and high spirits just by walking into the room. Of all the medical personnel, she was the most natural with him, and since she didn't distort or simplify her speech, he could easily understand her. The two of them bantered about how much Coke he was sneaking. To me she said, "If you're making that apple pie tomorrow, I'm not on 'til three." Many of those nurses I admired so much are still friends.

They were all colorful. One of the night-shift nurses always did a wild interpretation of a villain for Carlos—a kind of Mississippi River desperado who twirled the curled tips of his infamous moustache with an eye roaming shiftily, on the lookout for trouble. After the elaborate, never-changing charade, wonderfully out of keeping with her silver hair and grandmotherly manner, she'd point to Carlos and laugh longer and louder than anyone in the room.

One night there was no twirling of the sinister moustache, and Carlos asked, "Why you quiet?" She tried to break into her old routine, but she couldn't make it work.

"Something matter?" Carlos asked softly.

"No," she said pertly. Then unexpectedly she sat down on the hospital bed beside him. It was a wonderful hospital for not enforcing rigid rules about who could be on the beds.

"I am thinking about the girl across the hall," she said. It was almost the first time she'd talked to him rather than mimed her one performance.

"What happened?" Carlos asked.

"She had a second transplant. The kidney stopped working last night, and she's been crying all day."

I watched his face, watched him look out the window and up into the mountains for a long time. I could see the nurse wondering whether or not she should have told him about it. When he turned back to her, "How old?"

"Fourteen," the nurse answered.

Carlos looked stricken. "She's too young," he said. He wrote her a note I didn't see and asked the nurse to take it to her with one of his bouquets of flowers.

That night he too was quiet, and I again left him earlier than usual. Between then and morning he wrote his account of all that had befallen him since he'd been ill.

"Moody in two ½ year"

In 1975 in summertime I went to see counselor for the School for the Deaf. I ask him I want to see Doctor. Jim said what you need Dr. for? I said, "I throw up and sick all the time." So he write little note and give me Dr.'s address. Few day I went to see Dr. He check my body and blood pressure. Dr. was very surprise. He say I have high blood pressure—over 200. The Dr. call Jim. I don't know what they talk about.

Next day I am go to see Jim again. He explain to me. I feel upset. I left from Jim's office. Few month I went to another Dr. at McKay Dee Hospital. He say, "You still have high blood pressure." He want me to stay in the hospital for one week.

When I was asleep, I dream about devil. I should almost dead in the hospital because when I woke up it was really hard breathe and my heart hurt and pain. So I call nurse. They not know nothing. So next day I ran down on 35th Street near Adams Street. I saw my mother and I call her.

She and I was arguing. Lilly want me back in the hospital. I said "No, I want to go home." So Lilly won't take me home. She drove me down McKay Dee. I was mad. The Dr. was check my body. He say he not know nothing what to do. Next day I am out of hospital.

Few month I bother Jim. I told him I still sick and weak and throw up. I was upset and cry. Few week Jim take me in to the nurse home in Murray by Salt Lake City. Two week later Jim and I went to U. of U. Hospital. Dr. check my body, but he really know. He told be two more year I will be dead. He give me some pills for blood pressure. I left U. of U. Hospital.

I was unhappy because I am short life, that's why. Jim take me back home. I can't stand my mother's house. I left. I am go see my friend. I live with him. I start smoking pot and drink every day. I am going risk my life. My friend was mad because I don't pay for rent and not help. So he kick me out. Few week there was another operation on my left arm. Jeri watch and interested. She look at my arm. I try to look at my arm. They said, no. I don't feel my arm. It like dead arm. I stay in the hospital for one week. Dr. told me when I go home they explain I have to go to Center for dialysis, three time a week for four hour. I hate it.

I start dialysis on July 30. I am not happy about it. One time I refuse go Dialysis Center. Cammie and Tom came to my apt. They was worried about me. They ask me, "Will you go to dialysis today?" I said, "Okay, I will." They left, that's all. On Sept. I plan for transplant. Robert and I and Nancy meet about it. She said, "No transplant because Robert have something wrong." I feel lousy. Few month Jeri and I went to Las Vegas, Nevada. Someone call. They want know where am I. They found and call Jeri about transplant. It is too late. Jeri and I talk about it.

Next month I went to dialysis. Nancy call Jim at dialysis (another Jim). Nancy ask, "Carlos is there?" Jim S. said yes. After dialysis, Jim ask me, "Why you want it?" I told him I am big risk life, and I care. He said nothing. I left dialysis room, but I was always little too scared to have a transplant. Anyway I went to U. of U. Hospital. Nancy check my blood, then I get bath. Then on bed. They get me down to operation room. I hug Jeri and Linda. Linda said, "Are you scared?" I told them I care dead or alive. She said nothing.

Operation was over. I feel well with my new kidney. Three week later and I feel lousy and pain. I feel I want to go bathroom, but I can't. It is pain and hurt. Dr. take me for X-ray. They found something wrong. I have to get another operation. Next day when I woke up, I look my body. On my right leg was pharmaseal bag for urine, and a very tiny tube in my stomach. It is for old kidney. For about two week, then finally it is off. Other off, both.

Now how I feel about new kidney? Well, I think I am little glad, but it is very dangerous. I know it is not easy life, but I will careful with myself. I hope it is work long and long time. I am glad I don't have to go to dialysis. If the kidney won't work, I will v7#/%X!

"My father was gone on the earth."

ONE OF THE MOST FASCINATING moments in my life with Carlos was when he sat in his hospital bed and pored over the blue scrapbooks I had kept over the years I'd known him. There were the pictures he had pilfered from his mother's collection that I shamelessly retained, the countless notes and drawings, the occasional entreaties and apologies, the million thanks. Among the pages was some of his schoolwork, which he now turned to and studied closely, every sentence. He smiled in amusement and probably wonder at his having done any of it at all.

Suddenly he looked up at me with a solid pride in himself and said, "My teacher's wrong!" I came over to stand by his bed where I could see the page he was looking at. He flipped ahead several pages and back several more. "And wrong! *She* was *ladzy*!" That had been Marian's favorite phrase for him: "You're lazy!" she would say, prodding him into a little more work. And now he loved to turn the tables. First, he had found a line in a story where "Valentine's" was misspelled. He had gone on in his story to say, "My teacher will make twenty-four pink cookies for us." Knowing her very well by now, he looked at me and said, "Wrong! She bought them."

He found other errors here and there—the *a* left out of Tuesday, a page of additions with two incorrect sums that had escaped the red pencil. And best of all, a sentence in which he was to fill in the blanks: Sally said her name was _______________ _______________. In both blanks, Carlos had gotten away with writing "Sally."

What I remembered in the hospital as I watched Carlos examine his earlier work was the boy who had had to use all the determination he could summon while copying a story over, or adding and re-adding columns of numbers, or working at his speech until his heart burned with the hopelessness of being understood. To see him sit in his bed and fastidiously examine his work, finding the errors his teachers had missed, or more likely simply let go, was like watching a flower bloom, the amazing unfolding of all its intricacies almost surpassing comprehension. Now he was able to say to the nurses, who couldn't leave him alone, "*Please* (this uttered with the sweetness and piety of an altar boy) let me have *one* Coke." When the answer came back, "Not for two more hours," he would implore, "I have not had twenty-five hundred cc's yet."

During our visits Carlos lay in bed or sat up in a big reclining chair as he told me about his childhood. He always had on blue-and-white pajama bottoms, institutional right down to the drawstrings. But the faded brown T-shirt was all his own. It was hot in the hospital, and he had cut it down to nothing in order to cool himself a bit. Gone were sleeves, neckband, and five inches of waist. He was still a very young man, lying there in his striped bottoms and funny top, but he was passive and gray and gentle now. Only occasionally did a few feathers of the wild and vigorous bird he had been flutter through his days.

In the years we were remembering, he had swooped into school, late usually, creating his own energy field wherever he went and dominating it entirely. What a contradiction he had been, with his manner of a dauphin who meant to have his day before he ascended to the throne, but who, in the doing, would never misunderstand his legacy. He had been all leap and dash with his mint breath and daisy heart and forest eyes that came to know everything.

When Carlos and I were together, he wanted particularly to tell me about the years in which I hadn't been at the edge of his life. "All the time left, left my mother's," he said once. He was thoughtful when I asked him why. "Meybe looking for trouble. Trouble, trouble, all the time trouble." When these flashes of his early days came to mind, I sometimes found myself longing for his old wildness to exercise myself against. He did know how to try me.

"Well, I don't remember my first friend. I guess Manuel my friend, because he live close my house," Carlos wrote after I had begged and bribed him daily to jot down more about what he remembered of his early days. "Manuel and I was with for twelve years," he told me.

"Did you want trouble?" I asked.

"No," he said, and I believed him. "Learned from my friends."

He told me about the first time he'd stolen anything, a subject he had either avoided or flaunted at the time it made up a big part of his life. I guess I was a little surprised to find that he had ceased regarding it as a great feat. "Me, Manuel and Frank stole potato chips, bought beer and ran over the hill." Apparently Frank ended up on a bike and "the cops caught him and he told them the names of his friends, Manuel and Carlos. We had to work for eight hours," he recalled. I watched him relive it in his mind. "Me and Manuel mad at him," he added, his mood darkened.

One night he handed me the portfolio he'd been writing in. I thought he'd written more about his friend Manuel, but when I came to it, that page was just as it had been. Following it was a page that dazed me. I understood that it was an outline of his life, but the numbers—7825? I read it and re-read it, wondering where the idea for it could have come from.

7825 I get new kidney
7724 Linda & me are unhappy. But still unhappy
7623 I married Linda
7522 I get bad health for my kidney
7421 I am finish my school
7320 My son Charlie. Last time I see him 2½ month old
7219 should I marry Cathy but I drop it.
7118
7017 First time I meet Cathy R.
6916 I start learn drug. I habit pot but still

6815
6714 I went to Montreal Ca with Jeri
6613
6512 I was learn how to steal learn through by friend
6411 I was trouble in school
6310 Jeri and I was Freind
629
618 I watch TV Superman
585
574
563
552 my Father was gone on the earth
541

Finally I looked away from the page long enough to ask him about the numbers. "Here—1978," he said. "I am twenty-five. I get new kidney." There was little doubt about his disappointment in my ability to read a simple history, but I had been too amazed at what he'd contrived to do to crack his system.

Somewhere inside himself in the interminable night hours, he'd run his mind over and over the delicate backbone of his uncommon life. In its tight reduction of a year to a line was the poetry, the whimsy, the confusion and sorrow, and the grand adventure of one boy's quarter of a century. As I read it, I was struck again by his use of language. "My Father was gone on the earth," he had written for 1955, the year he was two.

Deaf, disadvantaged in a thousand subtler ways, still he was able to create a world, and almost a language, of his own.

"My life was down. I will bring it up."

I HAD PLENTY OF OPPORTUNITY to notice that Carlos's remaining months were the gentlest, and in many ways the most giving, of his life. I wondered if they were satisfying to him in the way they were to those of us who admired what he had become. I asked him in one of our last conversations, partly because I wanted a chance to tell him how much I respected him.

"You've been wonderful right through everything," I said to him during a hospital visit. "I've never liked you better or enjoyed you more. How is it for you? Any good?"

"No," he answered. I don't know why I was surprised—I guess simply because I wanted the answer to be different. Lilly had said to me recently, "No one has suffered more than Carlos." She was right. How could I have hoped that the years in which he had twenty-two surgeries would be good?

He saw that his candid answer distressed me, and, nudging my arm, added, "But it's okay."

"Why no?" I asked. It was one of those stupid questions of mine that I wished I could call back. I started to apologize the moment I asked it, but he was already responding.

"Because bad luck with sick," he said, as straightforward as a weather report. He had an unfailing ability to keep self-pity from such a conversation.

"In spite of everything, you've been loved, and you've been loving all your life," I told him. "And now more than ever. Not everyone has that, or gives that. And you've been handsome and smart, and wise as well."

"Wise?" he asked.

"More than smart. Able to understand what it all means," I said. "I'll give you an example, and this is just a little thing compared to other things you do. I'm impressed that you don't use drugs anymore." It was one of his most articulated renunciations. He'd seen many of those closest to him damaged and often ruined by using and selling drugs. I remembered the sign in his kitchen with its stark message, six inches high: DON'T DO DRUGS. That couldn't have been popular with more than half the friends who came by to visit him. He had been in circles where he could have made a great deal of money in drugs, and he had chosen not to.

He lay so still and quiet, so without rancor or resistance that it made my heart ache for what his fate had been. "You never asked me or anyone to bear your burdens for you," I said. "That made it easy to be with you. And to love and admire you."

He became more introspective and thoughtful about his life in the last year. His sister Miranda, whom I'd liked enormously, had given him a book about positive living, and I always saw it at his home in Ogden when I was there. He told me he read it very slowly, "everything two times," looking up "many, many words."

"What are you learning from it?" I asked him on one of my visits to his place.

"God wants you to care," he said.

"That's a beautiful sentence, Carlos—a beautiful thought." It occurred to me that he had never tried to change anything about me. He was speaking for himself; there was no recruitment in it.

"I read it in my book," he said. There was something pure in heart in Carlos, and it always touched me.

"And you're going to church. How did you pick one?" The one he'd chosen happened to be mine, but I'd never made a case for it. He thought for a moment. Always in such situations, I felt the anticipation of hearing what his ideas would be. I looked at him, waiting.

"More deaf people there," he said.

"That's a good reason," I answered, and I laughed at how he could combine intents.

I'd gone to church with Carlos in one of the stretches of time when he was out of the hospital. I remember looking over to see him signing as everyone else sang "Abide with Me." That's when I began fervently summoning the powers of whatever heaven there is to make gentle the last days of this valiant man, now thirty-four years old. He looked elderly standing there in the congregation. He was stooped, he weighed eighty pounds, one knee was crippled from arthritis. He was losing his hair. And he shone.

I asked about his churchgoing a few weeks later, still intrigued, and he said one of those sentences of his. "My life was down," he told me, lowering his hand. Then, reversing the motion, he added, "I will bring it up."

I called Marian that night. "'My life is down. I will bring it up,' Carlos told me." She was silent. I knew what she was feeling. "What he knows," I finally said. "What do we know about language? What are the questions we'd ask?"

"Where does the language come from—that's what I'd like to know. And the ideas? Not whether deep structure had it right—which it didn't."

"Another contingent of linguists is saying we store by analogy—the brain has an endless capacity for analogy."

"Of course it does. They did get that right."

"The physicists are saying maybe time plays backward. Better than time is running out."

"And they're surprised?" she said.

"So our memories are in the future."

"You've always been a backward-looking creature—whatever they're called."

"At least not a lemming."

"Not much of a lemming."

"I like to think time is playing backward. Does it give him more of a chance?"

She didn't answer, and I said, "He is still so poetic."

"Some of the poetry was in being almost right. 'I will spring at the Saturday.' He knew it was wonderful. He might not have known why."

"We couldn't bring ourselves to correct him. How would you correct 'I will spring at the Saturday'?"

"He operates on more than the novelties of 'almost right.' Plenty of other deaf kids weren't being quoted for their charm or originality."

"'My life is down. I will bring it up.'"

"Tell him hello."

"I will."

"You can't fly."

ONCE, WHEN I came to visit Carlos, his eyes were full of the devilment of his early years. He was back in the hospital again, and he lifted the white sheet and glanced at the scar across his lower abdomen and obviously at what was in the vicinity. When he looked up at me, he said, "I'm a little boy again."

He was laughing, but I was afraid there was some somber news behind his jesting. Whatever did he mean? Had the manhood of his young years left him already?

"What are you talking about?" I finally laughed, caught up in his fun.

He made me wait, enjoying the concern he could see he'd roused, before he finally said, "No hair."

"Still? After a month?" I laughed again. "Well, what the hell, who needs it?" I loved his being one of the few who could keep his manhood and not lose his boyhood, whatever circumstances brought to him.

Carlos woke up from a nap one day to see me sitting beside him. "My body's almost a monster," he said to me, rubbing his eyes and stretching. I couldn't believe what I'd heard.

"What about your body?" I questioned.

"My body's almost a monster," he said again, knowing he had both an idea that was funny to him and a sentence that was sophisticated.

It *was* funny the way he said it, arms extended to offer his body as the necessary evidence. It was I who was trite and predictable. "Your body is beautiful," I said.

"No. Wrong," he replied. "Look," and he gave me a tour, beginning with the purple rings on the backs of his hands, then moving to the scars on both arms, the fistula that vibrated like a little bee inside where the vein and artery had been joined. He went on through the scars on both legs, lingering on the one where the shunt had been. He pointed out the scars from the surgeries the transplant had required and ended with the hated urine bags. A nurse had dropped one in the main corridor of the hospital one day while she was taking him for an X-ray. "Awful," he came upstairs saying.

I laughed at him, we laughed together about the injustices his body had suffered. He had learned to apply his wonderful humor to the most macabre aspects of his situation, and it lifted us both beyond them.

"You don't ever get sad about it anymore. You don't cry. Everybody on both sides of you and across the hall is crying half the time," I said to him. "You're falling behind."

"I don't care," he said softly, and I knew he meant *I don't let the care ruin me.* And then he added, "Better when we talk."

He was in a chatty mood, and that evening he said, "You know why I'm not live at home for four years?" Then he ran his fingers over the bedsheets as fast as he could move them, his hand speeding along to the edge and then dropping off.

"What's that?" I asked. He was as funny as ever when he did those imitations he was famous for.

"Rats and roaches," he said. "I hate thees."

That night as I left, he said, "I'm welling."

"What?" I asked "And why such lousy speech?"

I couldn't be made to understand and finally he reached for his always nearby paper and wrote, "Welling. If you house own—when you die, maybe you give someone."

"Will!" I exclaimed. Talking with him was like being on a treasure hunt. There was a kind of jubilant discovery in understanding him. "You *will* your things to someone. It's not the same as 'I will come to see you at noon.'"

"Meybe my old radio," he said, whose arching, golden wood I am looking at as I write this. He gave me a tight hug and pronounced an almost ceremonial, "Thank you for coming." As I drove home that night, my mind fell back to an incident that had happened before Carlos came into the hospital for the transplant. He had driven me to the airport one sunny afternoon, and we had had lunch together in the terminal restaurant. It was the kind of time I had come to cherish with him. Sometimes we said funny things and amused ourselves outrageously, but not always, or even usually. We had moved into a quiet, contented state, marked by the kind of familiarity—almost dailiness—that provides the deep rudder to life's turbulence.

I had no wish that moment to walk away from the sanctuary of caring for each other, no thought of a plane to catch, or another life to get to. That other life was more than good, but Carlos was a thing apart. He stayed so connected, and he brought me into the circle of his beneficence. But I did walk down the corridor, Carlos beside me, until we came to the gate and he leaned to kiss me, delicately as a bird might.

"Don't let your plane down," he said just before I boarded, making it crash into the ground with his hands.

"If it does, I'll spring out and fly to the sun—I'll singe my wings, waiting for you." I demonstrated as I spoke.

But he was serious, the parent for a moment, all knowing and sadness, protective of my ingenuousness. He looked at me and said, "You can't fly."

"I'll try though," I answered, not flapping my would-be wings now but smiling at him. I thought suddenly of a friend of mine who had said of him, "Poor kid, what has he ever had?"

"More than most of us," I had answered.

"I'll try," I repeated that day that now seems like another lifetime ago, knowing how many skies I'd batter my wings in for Carlos Louis Salazar.

"For love."

AS CARLOS BECAME more and more able to manage his world, I slowed down what had become almost a campaign where he was concerned. It allowed me to take the kind of look that lets the weights shift. Now that he was strong, I could be if not weak, at least reflective for a moment. Actually I felt awash in weakness and fear.

Our days were filled with smiles and sometimes our old hilarity, but I avoided looking ahead. While he was doing better emotionally, he was not gaining ground physically. On the contrary, his chemistry numbers were diving about; he was harder and harder to stabilize. He was going into surgery again, and still he had infection. What else lay ahead for him?

One night I leafed through the scrapbooks I'd made of Carlos and the piles of notes, letters, keepsakes that had been tossed on top of them. What I found there pulled me into the sharp focus Carlos was best at leading me to. Through my collection was a kind of self-indulgence Carlos had never allowed himself. I looked again at his four drawings and wondered in what various and limiting ways those of us who have the luxury of easily acquired language misspend it.

Though it was almost dark, I drove back up into the foothills and to the hospital. But instead of going in, I walked my familiar route to Red Butte Canyon. The buttercups were closing their petals and I saw a monkshood. How can something so beautiful be poisonous? I leaned against a large rock, still warm from the day, and lost myself in the companionship of trees.

It was rough coming down the trail in the dark, and when I got out of the brush, I was scratched up. I was tired, but I wasn't at all sleepy—I felt a kind of nervous liveness. I knew a big component of it was apprehension. By the time I got to the hospital, I'd straightened myself out a little.

As I walked through the glass doors and toward the bank of elevators that led to Carlos's room, I stopped at the pay phones and took out the little red address book I carried in my purse. The card Dr. Rachel Remen had given me almost ten years earlier was still in my wallet. I dialed the number, and as the phone rang, I recalled her telling me, "If you come to a place where you don't know what to do, call me."

I remembered Mark Twain saying somewhere that everyone is a little bit insane at night. Then Rachel's voice was on the line and I talked. I began telling her of my dark-eyed boy, his early wild-hearted living, the past months strung with red tubes, and the present borne down with the shadow of foreign masses in his struggling body. And yet were his wings clipped now or was he just beginning to soar?

"Why was he born?" she asked softly.

Oh, there was reason, so terribly much reason everywhere I looked, whatever segment of his life I took up—from his leaps in the sunflowers to his running frantic and lost in the foothills and coming back, always coming back—there were reasons time without end for Carlos.

"What is his purpose?" she asked, again.

And again I was still, watching in my mind the ancient human struggle of a boy coming to understand himself, and to move beyond his limitations. It was all against the odds for Carlos, yet triumph is the word that most comes to mind in thinking about his life. Without having heard language, he was a phrasemaker. Without having had an advanced education, he became sophisticated in the most wonderful sense of the word. Without having had health, he lived fully and deeply. Without having had a merciful life, he was compassionate. Without having had money, he brought riches. With so much to endure, he did endure.

Again a question. "What are the qualities unique to him?"

He danced before my eyes as rare and brilliant as a field of wildflowers.

Wherever he was, and in whatever condition, he provided a gathering place for laughter and camaraderie. Once he had surprised me with the gift of a miniature cast iron stove like the one my grandmother had had in the cabin at the sawmill. "Why are you giving me a present?" I asked.

"For love," was his answer.

Again Rachel asked a question and waited. "Has he finished?"

For the first time in looking at his altered life, I could acknowledge the possibility that he might have, but that I didn't know, I wouldn't know.

She asked a last question. "What is the worst thing he can lose now?"

I knew it wasn't his life.

Rachel said it better than I ever could have. "Your work, Jeri, is to take care of his spirit, to keep him close to his identity. That's your part. Keep seeing his strength, his spirit, and reflect these back to him. You must say to yourself, 'I am a friend of this young man's soul. How am I going to let that help him keep what he is?' Use your knowledge of this man. You have the piece that no one else has."

I thought of Carlos sitting in the airport with me a few months earlier, talking and smiling and then his eyes turning to concern at the gate as he said, "Don't let your plane down." Seeing the images of him that danced before me was like running my hands through the jewels that had come to mind as I'd watched him learn language.

"Turn to the things that give you comfort and you will know the way," my friend said as we told each other goodbye.

A gathering peace settled over me. Hadn't we found our way to that preservation? The taking care of that amazing essence? And wasn't that the chance we'd been given? I walked back outside. It had begun to rain, and I looked up into the foothills. I could see a faint, light line where the rain was turning to snow.

If Carlos had been dash and verve, now he was something more. He was the triumphant in the face of the tawdry, cruel facts of life. Once again he had been the one waiting to meet me in that realization. What was, was. It would stand.

acknowledgements

Heartfelt thanks to Alice Peck who brought friendship as well as fine editorial skills to this endeavor. She is a beautiful intermediary between the world you're in and the world your story comes from.

Special thanks to Duane Stapp, bold and graceful designer, whose tools include elegance and generosity along with astonishing talent.

Profound thanks to the ever-buoyant Cill Sparks for her faith in this book, for her careful and indispensable readings, and for her sustaining friendship.

Many thanks to Ruth Mullen, indefatigable copyeditor and adventurer in the quest for perfection and to Arthur Goldwag, who understood the song and spoke for it.

Thanks to David Kranes, early and untiring mentor, keeper of the deepest faith between friends.

Special thanks and tribute to the Salazar family, who took me in.

Remembering William Mulder, who taught me to read and to reach.

about the author

Jeri Parker grew up scrambling along riverbanks and forest paths in Idaho. She spent summers with her grandparents at a sawmill that was a few miles from Yellowstone National Park.

She taught high school and university students for many years, but it was when she met Carlos Louis Salazar, a ten-year-old deaf boy that she began to understand what language is and what the intricate steps of acquiring it involve.

Publications include *Uneasy Survivors: Five Women Writers* and poems and short stories in literary reviews. Jeri is an artist as well as writer. Her paintings are in private and public collections in Paris, Athens, Frankfurt, Istanbul, London, Sydney, and more than half of the states. One of the first works she did was a pencil portrait of Carlos.

She is presently co-owner of Wildflowers Bed and Breakfast. Her own domain is ruled by a spaniel, two cats, and five golden chickens.